The Dream of Icarus:
My Journey into Paramotoring

By Lloyd Twelves

Contents

Introduction .... - 1 -

So, you dream of flying? .... - 5 -

My very first taste of flight .... - 8 -

Dreams seldom shout .... - 12 -

First morning of school .... - 15 -

First afternoon of school .... - 19 -

Looking for an eagle but finding a mountain goat .... - 23 -

Upgrading my surf board to a jet ski .... - 29 -

Paraglider to paramotor transition .... - 35 -

Not all wings are created equal .... - 39 -

Practice makes perfect .... - 43 -

Further progression and tandem flight .... - 47 -

First solo flight .... - 53 -

Versatility of flight .... - 61 -

Speed is irrelevant .... - 67 -

Set backs .... - 70 -

Doubts .... - 75 -

Risk and risk perception .... - 81 -

Coming back .... - 86 -

Going it alone .... - 90 -

Flying buddies .... - 94 -

Droning on .... - 98 -

Noisy neighbour? .... - 102 -

Shake, rattle and hole .... - 111 -

Taste of a millionaire lifestyle?	- 117 -
Fly-ins and flying holidays	- 127 -
Flying cars?	- 135 -
'Adventure flying' or 'bivouac' trips	- 140 -
Points for the budding pilot	- 146 -
How do I get started?	- 150 -
Tips on buying equipment	- 155 -
Final thoughts	- 160 -

Introduction

Let me be completely upfront with what this book is, and indeed what it is not.

This is an outline of my own personal experiences about fulfilling one of man's oldest dreams; that of personal flight. *Actual* flight that is, not sitting in a machine whilst moving through the air, but moving through the sky with nothing below your feet but the Earth; feeling the air on your face; reaching out and touching, and even tasting, clouds; with no metal cocoon restricting your view and diluting the experience. Herein I will explain my own path to the sport of paramotoring, the adventures I have had along the way, some of the pitfalls with which the budding pilot might learn from my mistakes, and the warm and helpful people that help to make this activity so great.

If you have ever dreamt of flight as a child (or indeed an adult!), are a little susceptible to 'cloud-watching' and are always the first to fight for the window seat when travelling in a plane, then this book is for you. Have you ever watched exhilarating videos online of aerial daredevils and thought 'that looks great; I wish I had the opportunity to try something like that!'? Or simply watched in bemusement as a local paramotor pilot flies over your house and wondered why that man was strapped to a giant desk-fan, then I hope you will enjoy this book and learn a little something about this fantastic pastime.

What you will be introduced to is an affordable form of powered flight. If you believe owning your own powered aircraft is restricted to the realms of the super-rich, with visions of helicopter pads and private jets, then you are not alone. Gladly however, I am here to tell you this is not the case. Small enough to fit in the back of most cars, no heli-pad or runway needed, a paramotor offers you the flexibility to go and float around the clouds after a hard day at the office as the ultimate way to unwind. If that sounds a little too sedate, the same equipment can be used to pull off incredible acrobatic manoeuvres, hitting over two 'G' in tight turns, and yes, even going upside down. The flexibility of these aircrafts still amazes me.

Some of you may be inspired to listen to that inner whispering voice which urges you to follow your dreams of flight and realise that, yes, it is within reach. I truly hope this aids in both outlining some of the introductory answers, dismisses fears and doubts you may have about 'being able to', but more importantly learning from my experience and perhaps saving you time, money or even injury.

Which leads me to clearly state what this book is not...

This is not meant in any way as a guide or 'manual' to teach yourself how to fly a paramotor. If this is your aim, to be blunt, you are being foolish. Would you read a book on how to drive a car and then jump into the driving seat? How would you feel if after boarding your international flight on an aeroplane you discovered the pilot had taught himself by reading a book; even if it was a *really* detailed book, and never had any one-to-one tuition? Good luck with that.

To this end, whilst I will naturally give an overview of the equipment involved, and some of the things to look out for when purchasing your gear, I will intentionally leave out details on precisely *how* to fly a paramotor. It would be irresponsible of me to put down in a book the processes of flying an aircraft in sufficient detail so a novice can read it and feel confident enough to forego specific training and tuition. These are aircrafts which can be bought relatively cheaply online, with no licensing requirements, and provide the ability to launch from your local field (or even your back garden if it is large enough!) and so I want nobody's injury, or worse death, on my conscience.

There are a handful of books out there already that go into detail around the mechanics of how these aircraft fly, the proper maintenance required, and an overview of how to fly them. These supplement a training course with a qualified instructor very well, and this book is in no way a challenge to these resources.

At the end of the book I will outline some steps to 'getting started' so if you have felt inspired to consider the sport for yourself then you will know how to begin.

I myself am not affiliated to any product or brand, nor am I greatly experienced. I wouldn't even suggest I have natural talent for the sport. As you will come to learn, I had to work very hard learning the skills required to be a competent paramotor pilot; I was not a 'natural'. With hindsight this is probably a benefit, as I will gladly trade short-term frustration for long-term safety and happiness.

At the time of writing, I have just over 3 years of solid experience, having amassed several hundred flights. There are those out there who have been having fun on these things for over 20 years, but I believe that the best way to learn is from someone who is still making the odd mistake, and can still view these aircraft with a youthful vibrancy and enthusiasm for what they can do and the opportunities they can bring to your life.

To reiterate, this is not intended as a master class. This is my personal journey, the destination having not yet been reached...

So, you dream of flying?

It is paradoxical, but somewhat undeniable, that mankind has always wanted to fly. For a species bound to the earth, with no natural manner with which to attain flight, this does strike me as a particularly cruel trick of Mother Nature. Perhaps it is the seemingly impossible nature of it that has drawn so many towards it's pull.

Want proof of this claim? Think no further than many religious or mythical figures where the God's live in the heavens, amongst the clouds, whilst demons and mankind toil on or under the earth. It appears as no coincidence to my mind that Zeus, King of the Gods in ancient Greek mythology, just so happens to be depicted high in the sky, hurling his lightning bolts at those below him. Not to mention the story of Icarus who, instructed by his father, went so far as to strap feathered wings to himself in order to attain flight. This story, and the imagery it provokes, has always resonated with me strongly - so much so that I have used it as the namesake of this book.

Nor does this pattern appear to have left us as time has moved on. In modern day fiction, almost every superhero can either fly, or come close to flying via swinging from rooftops. Modern iconography often depicts the eagle as a symbol of power, with many great nations or even sports teams choosing this as their emblem, and of course it is the penthouse apartment, sitting atop the rest, which commands the greatest prestige and therefore the highest price.

Take a brief moment to visualise your dream house. It's size, shape, dimensions and location. I'm prepared to bet most will imagine a home with far reaching views of a landscape or seascape below them, enjoyed from a high vantage point such as a cliff or hill-top.

The ability to live up high, to fly, to travel without boundary, has always been a desire of mankind's and remains synonymous with, above all, *freedom*.

Freedom from what exactly is perhaps more personal. The ability to float away and leave your troubles behind? To transcend gravity's pull and leave life's worries 'down there'? Or simply a rebellious strike against natures limitations and facing what can be for some, a great fear? The fear of heights, or falling, is not uncommon. Gladly, as I will go on to explain, most of the sensations associated with falling are eradicated when flying a paramotor, although I won't pretend it doesn't take a good dose of courage for that first solo flight.

Many before us have been limited by the technology of their age. Truly therefore, we live in blessed times when personal flight is attainable. Many of the people I speak to about the subject of flying often use words such as 'privilege' or 'humbling' when discussing their own experiences of flight, correctly recognising that it is still rare enough to feel special.

If this resonates with you, I urge you to continue reading, and perhaps let me open your eyes to a new world. A beautiful new world that already exists, directly above your head, if you only have the impetus to travel there.

Before we dive into my story, I will leave you with one of my favourite quotes:

"For once you have tasted flight you will walk the earth with your eyes turned skyward, for there you have been and there you will long to return."

None other than Leonardo da Vinci spoke these words. Limited by the technology of his age, it is enlightening to hear that one of the greatest imaginative minds of all time found flight, and the freedom it represents, to be a burning desire. Thankfully, we need not rely on our imaginations as Leonardo did, but can follow up our dreams with action. If this book has any aim, it is to prompt you to do just that.

My very first taste of flight

Most people have their first taste of flight, such as it is, in commercial aeroplanes. A rather muted experience; cramped spaces with only a glimpse of the sky through a small circular window. My experience was a little more unique…

It is the year 2000 and I am 14 years of age. Due to various factors, being raised in a single parent family for one, I had not previously had the opportunity to holiday abroad. This was not about to change for another 4 years, but whilst holidaying in Devon my Dad had arranged to meet a work colleague of his who owned his own 'micro-light' aircraft. I would later learn this was a 'flex wing' micro-light; ultimately a hang glider wing attached to a two-man bathtub on wheels.

We met my Dad's colleague at the local airstrip, and after introductions were over, we wasted no time in changing into 'flight suits' - ultimately thickly padded overalls, which oddly only seemed available in a selection of gaudy colours. From recollection, I chose a largely purple affair with golden accents as I thought this less emasculating than some of the other brightly coloured options. Nonetheless it did result in giving me a strong resemblance to a Cadbury's chocolate bar.

"I take it you have flown before?" the pilot asked me, as I was being strapped into a helmet with 'ear defenders' to protect from the noise of the engine.

I hadn't flown before. I remember being a little nervous about the possibility of getting motion induced sickness because I did suffer from travel sickness when in the back of a car as a young child. The truth was I simply did not know whether I was going to get along with the sensations of flying, or suffer from the fear of such extreme heights as some others do.

"A couple of times," I lied. This was simply too good an opportunity to miss, and I was worried that if I was honest with him he wouldn't want to be my experimental guinea pig pilot. Not in an aircraft where I would be sitting inches behind him and any possible gut-wrenching reactions on my part would be well and truly felt.

Before I knew it, I was sitting behind the pilot on a rather uncomfortable plastic seat, hurtling down the short grass runway on very small wheels which managed to find bumps that the naked eye could not discern. After being at what I assume was full throttle for a few moments, the pilot pushed the metal bar in front of him forward and I felt the sensation of leaving the ground for the very first time. That now familiar feeling in the pit of your stomach as you get hoisted into the air was, gladly, a thrill to me rather than a nauseating experience. Neither my stomach nor any related 'fear of flying' kicked in, and I simply loved the experience.

I remember very little about the flight itself. I couldn't tell you the sights I saw or how long it lasted, but I do have a very vivid memory of holding my arms out wide when I thought the pilot, seated right in front of me, was looking forward and wouldn't see this private moment whilst I pretend I could fly like a superhero. Naturally, he did eventually turn his head around and give me a quizzical glance, no doubt wondering why the teenager he barely knew was holding his arms out like an infant in order to enhance the experience. With good grace however, and much to my relief, he never pulled me up on it. Good guy.

This simple example really does highlight that many forms of flying are constrained by the aircraft in question. My introduction to the skies came in a more immersive form than most, but I still wanted to hold my arms out wide. I still wanted to see below me as we flew over landmarks, only to be restricted by the cocoon-like enclosure around me. From the passenger seat, being behind the pilot, even the view straight ahead was limited by the large round helmet that was inches from my face.

Later, I will explore and provide my thoughts on the different types of aircraft that I have experience of, and I shall leave it to you to decide which deliver what you are really seeking. For now, I shall continue with my back-story...

What would follow would be years of the usual; school and college, chasing (and largely missing) girls, drinking and reinventing what 'dancing' truly means. My first experience in a commercial aircraft came in the form of a group holiday to Spain at the age of 18. I'm sure I was thrilled by the chance of getting back in the air, although I can't recall too many details as the memories are somewhat hazy - for reasons I won't divulge here.

Dreams seldom shout

How many times have you been faced with an opportunity, no matter how small; to experience something or visit somewhere, and suddenly felt "oh yes, you know, that is something I've always wanted to try"?

I'm betting most of us have felt this at one time or another, but why is that? Why do we feel we have *always* wanted to do something but never found the time to actively pursue it? Mostly, I think, life simply gets in the way. The endless routine of waking up, getting ready, going to college / work, eating, commuting and sleeping, doesn't leave much room left for our passions or desires. The things we really want to do with our time rarely get prioritised.

It strikes me that our desires rarely grab our attention, certainly with no burning urgency of 'I really must do this'. Instead they lie dormant, often for years, only raising their little voices above the white noise of everyday life to briefly remind you that they are here. Such is the way of dreams it seems, and I would urge you to listen hard for the whispers of your own dreams and not let everyday life get in the way.

It was with my thoughts in this frame of mind, perhaps it was prompted by some TV show or another but I genuinely can't remember, that late one night sitting in the living room of my very first house (statistics have yet to prove, but I feel confident, that this was actually the smallest house in the western world), that something made me think of flying again. I remembered that first experience I had as an early teenager and the bold thought of actually owning your own aircraft, and flying it simply as a hobby, came back to me with full force. I had been working as a professional for a few years by this point, had very little savings but plenty of credit (welcome to my generation), and wondered just how affordable one of those micro-lights would be.

A short internet search later, past the images of multi-millionaires climbing into their helicopters, and I found a useful site about micro-lights. The upfront investment required to outright own one of these was well beyond my reach as a recent first-time home buyer. But the costs didn't end there it seemed; you needed a licence (ignoring the bureaucracy for a moment, this still requires time and money to study for); a local airport or at least airstrip to launch and land at; hangar fees (wait, so I pay money to have the thing sat there not being used?!) along with ongoing maintenance costs and it soon became apparent that this wasn't going to happen. Oh well, I'll just wait until I'm 50 or for my lottery numbers to come up I suppose.

But then I came across it; a stray link to another website offering a source of flying that appeared to actually be affordable. I had found my way on to a website for paragliding. Here they were, pictures of smiley happy people, young and fit, running off hill tops and souring to the clouds. I had found it! Not only affordable, but offering a great sense of that illusive *freedom* that flying represents. No cockpits; no clumpy flight suits; nothing below their feet but sky, and nothing above their heads but a thin cloth-like canopy.

I did a little research into the costs; a couple of thousand pounds upfront for the paraglider, or 'wing' as they called them, a helmet, and then the one-off costs of tuition. I already had some sturdy walking boots I could use. I read that I could pack the wing up into a large rucksack, throw it into the boot of my car, and launch from what appeared to be any random hillside. This was it – I was so excited about finding a flexible and affordable form of flying that I would have signed up there and then.

I found the most local school which could provide tuition, about half an hour's drive away in the UK's Peak District National Park, and I was booking my place before I had chance to think. I booked an 'Introductory Day', which promised to give me a taste of the action, and would count towards the full training course should I wish to continue to something called the 'Club Pilot's Licence'. Win–Win I thought.

First morning of school

"OK Peter, I'll see you Saturday."

I hang up having just booked my Introductory Day with Peter, the quietly spoken chap who is going to be teaching me paragliding. I am understandably excited, but my more immediate concern is finding the rendezvous point. You see, most paragliding sites are simply hill-sides, owned for the most part by local farmers whose entire 'holding' can be several acres.

Having never truly lived in the country, my rather innocent question of "could you give me a post code for the sat nav?" is instantly followed by Peter's mild laughter at the other end of the line. He gently explains that there is no post-code for a field and, in the absence of a neighbouring household next to the field, instead rattles off some directions which I hastily scribble down on some paper. The call ends and I review the notes. I am worried I should have asked for more clarity, because by the looks of it I seem to have been given directions to Mordor.

Continue past the village, leave the road and go down the dirt track.

Left at the big tree.

When there is a bend in the track, veer left and pass under the stone bridge.

Don't wake the troll.

Face east and say the magic words into the amulet.

Peter will appear on the nearby hilltop and teach me to fly.

The day arrives however and the directions serve. Soon I am parked up with around three others who are all here to fulfil a lifelong ambition. We meet in an open expanse of field surrounded by green hills and clear blue sky. The day promised to turn into what we English would describe as a 'scorcher'. Two of my fellow trainees are in their mid-twenties, like me, and one guy is clearly older, perhaps 60 or so. I meet Peter who is a friendly late-thirties / early-forties outdoor sort of chap, who smiles frequently from under a face with deep lines carved into it that can only be attained from years of being outdoors. Peter wastes no time in getting a school wing out of his car, laying it out on the ground and explaining the different components.

"These are the risers. A's go at the front with D's at the back."

"Make sure the lines aren't twisted."

"Notice the cell openings on the leading edge."

By the end of the first hour or so phrases such as 'angle of attack' were common place, and have no relevance to some judo stance - as would have been my first thought only hours earlier.

Without going into too much detail, a paraglider wing is basically a fabric canopy opened only at the front edge; not unlike an open envelope on its side. Passing the wing through the air, via running or the wind itself, inflates the canopy so it takes on a typical 'wing' shape. This special shape, referred to as an aerofoil, provides lift from creating a pressure differential in exactly the same way an aeroplane wing does. The fabric canopy is connected to the pilot via 30 or so 'lines' from all sections of the underside of the canopy. These 'lines' are typically made from Kevlar and are extremely strong, yet flexible; taking the weight of the pilot and connecting to the harness strapped around the pilot's mid-section via 'risers'.

After these introductions, the morning is spent doing one of the most important, and simultaneously frustrating, elements of learning to fly a paraglider – *ground handling*. A fancy phrase for what is basically kiting the wing above your head. It is a vital skill, and one that takes regular practice, given the start of any flight begins by getting the wing over your head and under your control.

Only this isn't a kite, it is a wing large enough to lift people off the ground, and when the breeze picks up you can really feel it try to lift you from under the harness strapped around your upper legs. That is, *when* it is directly over your head of course; which as a newbie seems to be the most difficult thing in the world. A pull on the risers and the wing comes up gently at first and then over-shoots; going overhead and falling behind you. Next time it comes up at one side and not the other; completely turning itself over in the process. The moments when you think you have it directly over your head, and are putting in the right amount of tension on the 'brake' handles to control the wing, are all too brief until you lose control of it again.

A solid hour of ground handling, when you are fighting the wing and moving around underneath it, forever looking up at the wing to ensure the centre mark is over your head and not to one side, is both exhausting and mesmerising. It turns out there's quite a bit of physical technique to controlling one of these wings, and I am heartened to see my fellow newbie's finding it just as difficult.

Peter is circling us one at a time, giving patient advice and helping to lay the wing back out after a failure. When the wind dies off, and we can't as easily ground handle, he is talking theory and answering our questions. Not a moment is wasted. This really is the reason why learning a skill demanding at least some physical technique cannot be gleaned from the pages of a book. One-to-one tuition is a must.

First afternoon of school

One thing you learn pretty quickly is that in order to launch a paraglider you must be facing into the wind. An aeroplane, for example, is typically limited by the layout of the runways (being classically in a cross or, better yet I'm told, a triangle formation) and so they are often not perfectly lined up to face directly into the wind. As such, planes take off with cross winds fairly regularly.

Given paragliders are much lighter than aeroplanes, they are more susceptible to wind direction. It is almost impossible to launch a paraglider in anything other than a direct headwind. Half of the trouble I was encountering with ground handling early on was basically trying to face the wing into wind where it is stable.

After eating our home-made sandwiches, our little group transfer to a different site for the afternoon session. Given the wind has died down a little by now, Peter gets on the phone to check out the weather using Apps and even phoning a friend of his who he knows will be out and about around the Peak District.

He settles on a location which is, and I quote, "a short drive away." We all pack up the wings, which in itself is not as carefree as you might imagine; each requiring vigilant folding so as to avoid damaging the 'cell walls' or the opened front edge of the wing. Following this, we each jump in our individual cars and set off following Peter. About 40 minutes later we are unpacking the wings again, but before we take them out of their respective bags, this time we have to walk them over fields, tracks, through gates and stiles in order to get to the site in question.

And the logic behind all of this travel? *To find an appropriate hillside that is facing into wind.*

You see, if the wind is blowing over the back of the hill, it creates unstable air which is difficult, and potentially dangerous, to try to launch from. If the wind is side on, as I have previously described, that is no good - you can't launch a wing without facing into the wind. So paragliders have certain 'sites' which must all be:

- Accessible, with permission of the landowner if necessary,
- Sufficiently steep,
- Some open or flat space on or near the top to lay your wing out,
- Decent landing field at the bottom, and
- Free of nearby obstacles (such as trees / buildings / cattle etc.)

... and on top of all that we need the above at multiple locations so as to face into most, if not all, wind directions!

Want to fly from that great south-facing hill near where you live? Then you had better hope for a wind coming from the South. What's that you say? It's a westerly wind today. Sorry bud; no flying for you!

Now it is probably true to say that as your experience grows, so too can more sites open up to you. A hill which doesn't have much flat space on the top would be unsuitable for a beginner but not necessarily for an experienced pilot, for example. I get that. Really I do. But travelling around, often miles in a car, every time the wind changes direction strikes me as a particularly frustrating element of what should be an activity about fun and freedom!

Happily, the wind remains in that direction for the rest of the day, and I get to experience my first 'hops' down a gently sloping hillside. Running from the top of the hill, the wing inflated and overhead, as the ground falls away my feet left the ground and I had perhaps 10 seconds of continuous flight and a very big smile on my face. All of my fellow newbie's are buzzing with the thrill of it also – we have finally flown, albeit briefly, just as we had all imagined when we were children.

Throughout the day I had gotten to know my fellow newbie's, in particular the older gentleman who, following retirement and looking for a new challenge, decided now was the time to finally take to the skies. It turns out that 'Trooper', as we nicknamed him (and like all good nicknames, once uttered forever sticks) was used to a life of action in his younger days, having served in the forces and lived in numerous countries during his time. He remarked that he was once sat with his wife on an outdoor bench, on some walking holiday around the Alps if I recall correctly, and out of the skies fell a paraglider who landed close to them. After exchanging pleasantries and hearing some reasoning for the abrupt entrance due to 'missing some thermals' he packed up his gear and was on his way.

That encounter left an impression on Trooper it seemed. A seed of ambition was planted; that one day he would give paragliding a go. He had to wait until his retirement to realise that dream, but here he was, a 60-odd year-old walking up hills and running of them again for the sheer joy of it. It was a great thing to witness and yet simultaneously, secretly, I was rather grateful I had the chance to try this well before I reached retirement age. I felt very thankful I had chosen to seek out the opportunity without too many years of yearning beforehand.

Looking for an eagle but finding a mountain goat

Over the next three months I continued to train with Peter. Working a regular office job during the week, I was limited to only the weekends in order to get my fix for what some might call an obsession. I would phone Peter up every Saturday morning for a weather check across the weekend and, this being England, was not always greeted with favourable news.

"It's a little too gusty today," Peter would say.

I would check my weather app, and see gusts of 15mph and reply "Really?"

With hindsight, I can tell you that paragliders are very much 'fair weather' aircraft. It is their largest drawback. They will technically fly in the rain, but much like cycling, why would you want to be exposed to the elements if it is raining? Actively falling snow is dangerous as it can potentially weigh down the fabric of your wing and you might stall – literally falling out of the sky when the wing loses its shape. Too much wind and the wing will drag you across the ground before you have had a chance to get it above your head - trust me, this hurts. In the months to come, I would take my own wing out on local playing fields near where I live, just to get more ground handling practice, but without due respect for how strong a 15mph breeze can be when you are attached to a wing that is the length of an average living room. Nowadays, if I see a gust over 12mph on the forecast I stay at home, save myself the bruises to both my body and my ego, and if I really have to I will even converse with relatives.

However, I would learn that too little wind can also be a hindrance to what is possible with a paraglider.

It was perhaps my fourth full day in the Peak District. I had ordered my very own wing by this point, having got some 'high flights' under my belt, whilst also sitting the odd exam. Yes, formal pen and paper questions to ensure I was learning the theory at the same time as the practical techniques. The first of these exams came after only the first couple of days, and in the absence of any classrooms in the middle of the National Park, was conducted in the front seat of my own car. Peter sat in the passenger seat, and I was presented with a paper of perhaps 20 or so multiple-choice questions that took all of 5 minutes to complete. The first question was: '*Now you have seen how much driving is involved to arrive at each hillside that faces into wind, are you sure you still want to fly a paraglider?*' To be honest I don't recall any of the questions, but certainly they weren't anything to worry about if you had been paying attention.

All the exams and training went towards what was called the Elementary Pilot's Licence ("EPL"). Next would come some more advanced techniques ('top landings', 'big ears', and other oddly named moves) across another 4 or so days before I would reach Club Pilot – the point at which you are deemed to be competent and not need a formal tutor present when you fly.

On this fourth day however, the wind disappeared. Not a fart of wind to be found. In such circumstances 'forward launching' is the only option which ultimately means that in order to compensate for lack of wind, you must run as fast as you can to generate the required 'air speed' to generate lift. It also has another implication; flights become pretty much limited to 'top-to-bottoms' only. Allow me to explain...

A paraglider can stay in the air for a long time by two primary methods: ridge soaring or catching thermals.

Ridge soaring is finding a wide hill, cliff face, or 'ridge' which faces into wind. As the wind hits this ridge, it is pushed upwards and so a paraglider can, by going back and forth along the ridge, remain in the updraft and therefore stay airborne for as long as the wind is constant. In little or no wind, this is not an option.

Thermals, on the other hand, are pockets of warm rising air. They are generated as the sun heats up different surfaces at different rates (so black tarmac would warm up faster than, say, a grass field) and as such the air around the surface is warming at different rates also. When these pockets of air become warmer than the surrounding air, they rise.

Have you ever seen a buzzard circling the skies, wings outstretched but not beating, and they appear to hold their height or go even higher? That is catching thermals, and paragliders can do the precise same thing.

The problem with catching thermals, assuming you have the correct weather conditions for a 'thermic' day, is that you can't see them. They are pockets or columns of rising air, so purposefully trying to find them is as much a question of chance as it is skill – at least at my level.

So back to my fourth day, and the only option is to run off the hills, hope to get lucky and catch a thermal (never happened) and land out at the bottom of the hill. Pick up your wing, throw it over your shoulder, and climb back up the hill – a 'top-to-bottom'.

It was whilst walking back up a hill with Trooper, my ego being bruised from being seemingly more out of breath than a man twice my age, that I noticed how Peter was himself walking up the hill in front of us. He appeared to be zig-zagging his way up the face of the hill, rather than, as Trooper and I were doing, walking up the hill in a straight line. To my simple, Romanesque mind this was silly; why was he adding unnecessary mileage to his journey?

I questioned his logic and he, like many experienced ramblers before him, was used to finding the easiest route, even if it was not the shortest. He was walking the path of least resistance, and his years of training people in the Peak District had meant he now did it without thinking. Trooper remarked how he was walking up the hills "like he was half man half goat", and that did get me thinking…

I had spent several days now in the lovely National Park, away from my girlfriend (who wasn't best pleased I was spending any given sunny weekend day away without her) and I had amassed a considerably short amount of 'air time'. I had however, spent time sat around on grass waiting for the wind to come on to the hill (often called 'para-waiting' by those in the community) and what seemed like far too much time walking up hills. My dream of flight appeared to be manifesting as a bloody walking holiday!

I would come back after one of these days, having spent what could easily be two hours in the car driving to and from the 'appropriate sites', utterly spent. A full day of unpacking wings, running off the hill tops, for what felt like moments in the air, only to be followed by traipsing back up the same damn hill to do it all again, is thoroughly exhausting. I was looking for an eagle to teach me how to fly, and I felt as though I had found a mountain goat who, knowledgeable and helpful though he was, was actually teaching me more about how to walk up hills.

I was starting to feel a little disillusioned with it all. Maybe the genuine personal flying I was looking for was not paragliding. Perhaps, as I had thought as a young adult, people required helicopters and jets to have any real chance of flight - and that was not to be found outside of a small lottery win.

Upgrading my surf board to a jet ski

Now I will freely admit, that in certain countries or specific locations, free flight paragliding is pretty much perfect. Look no further than videos online of people having long cross-country adventures in the Alps, where thermals are more common, ridges are longer, and the sheer size of the mountains means that even should they only do a top-to-bottom, they are getting some serious airtime.

If I lived in northern Italy, perhaps around Lake Garda where there is a cable-car operating all day taking tourists and paragliders to the top of 'Monte Baldo', then I would be thoroughly content with paragliding. I would have had the conditions for long flights and probably would not have looked any further.

However, I live in England, where even the so called 'Peak' District can only offer a highest point of just over 2000 ft above sea level ('Kinder Scout'). The Lake District, despite its name, does a much better job of offering some high mountains but not all of these are flyable, and let's not forget there is a reason it is called the *Lake* District.

So far, paragliding reminded me in many ways of surfing.

I had some grandparents who lived down in Newquay, and when I would travel down for a week every summer to spend time with my Dad in neighbouring Devon, we would always spend the odd day or so in Newquay so I could see my grandparents. Naturally, any trip to Newquay wouldn't be complete without the obligatory trip to the beach; mostly involving being sandblasted by the bracing winds coming off the Atlantic Ocean, huddling together for warmth as you watch the storms roll in… oh yes, good times. Once or twice I even tried my hand at surfing. Well OK, 'body boarding', but in my defence I didn't really spend the required time down there to gain any proficiency with genuine surfing.

I can however confidently say that, on what is widely considered one of the best locations in the British Isles to experience surfing, and being surrounded by proper surfers who could actually stay standing on a board, that surfing is an exercise in *patience*. You get changed into the requisite wetsuit, plod out into the freezing waves only to wait around, anxiously looking over your shoulder trying to judge if this next wave is sufficiently large enough to warrant your attempts at riding it. Mostly, the waves are not strong or wide enough, the ones that are present a coin toss of probability of you being skilful enough to properly 'catch it', and when you do you stay on for seconds at a time. Seconds!

I would watch the more experienced surfers, trying to pick up some tips of identifying the correct waves to gamble my pride on, but what I couldn't fail to notice was the duration of apparently successful catches. Even if they caught the wave well, followed it the correct direction and travelled the length of the wave - even they couldn't get more than 30 seconds of genuine, standing, surfing. They inevitably fall off, collect their board, and trudge right back out to wait around for the next 'golden opportunity'. Was I the only one who thought this was a poor exchange in the boring:fun ratio?

Paragliding was presenting very similar traits to surfing; limited time actually doing what you were there to do (surf / fly), reliant on favourable and rare weather conditions, and limited to a rather confined location. What if I wanted to surf over to those coves? No chance – you go where the wave is pushing you. What if I wanted to fly away from the ridge and up to that cloud? Then you had better hope you get lucky with the thermals, buddy.

Again, should you be fortunate enough to live in a handful of locations around the world that does regularly deliver the weather and surf conditions required, then I'm sure surfing is a great pastime. But ploughing your way through the waves only to turn around and have the waves push you back to the beach doesn't really feel like a joyous expression of freedom to me. Likewise, endlessly flying back and forth in front of the same hill quickly lost its appeal for me. What if, God forbid, I wanted to fly *over there*?

It was time to upgrade my surf board for a jet ski if I wanted to truly feel the liberty and freedom I was seeking when I dreamt of flying.

On occasions when we were para-waiting on the hills, once or twice the subject of paramotoring came up. I had never heard of it before, and we never saw one when I was there, but I was interested why there seemed to be general criticism of a sport which shared so much of the genetic make-up of paragliding. Peter didn't teach paramotoring, but had done it himself in the past. He described it as basically using a paragliding wing, but with the addition of a propeller strapped to your back, powered by a small petrol engine. He would describe it also as heavy, noisy, expensive, and portrayed a general feeling that using an engine to fly was somehow '*cheating*'. Some of the Club Pilots, who were on the same hill as us that day, would nod sagely in agreement; complaining that these paramotors would sometimes come over their way, buzzing past them while they themselves were waiting on the hills. I stayed silent on the clearly obvious counter-argument – that at least these paramotor pilots were flying, whilst others were sat on the ground waiting for the perfect conditions before they could get in the air.

I would later that evening look at pictures on the internet to find out more, and my first impression was one of disbelief. Imagine a large lawnmower powered desk fan strapped to your back and you get a good idea of the basic set up – it certainly did look ridiculous. How could anyone run with one of those on their back? Wasn't it dangerous to have an engine literally mounted to you, with a propeller spinning just inches from your head?

Despite these doubts, since I was becoming a little disillusioned with free flight paragliding, I continued to look online at videos of paramotoring, and what I found was jaw dropping. People flying not just to cloud base, but even above the clouds, and around them as though they were nature's own obstacle course laid out on the sky just for them. They could stay up there for as long as they wanted, not simply as long as some invisible thermal dictated. Next they would throw together some high powered acrobatic manoeuvres, spinning their wings upside down over and over (search *infinity tumbling* online and prepared to be amazed), only to use their engine's throttle to gain height when they had fallen too low, so they could do it all over again. I continued to watch, and found videos of people 'foot dragging' lakes and grass fields; flying so low that their feet were skimming the ground. As they had their own form of lift, in the form of an engine on their backs, they could do this for as long as they wanted. When they had to gain height again because they were approaching an obstacle, say a hedge, they simply squeezed the throttle in their hand and up they went! Not to mention that all the launches and landings were from flat open spaces; because they had their own form of thrust on demand, they didn't need hills in order to get in the air - they could take off and land from the same flat field. For someone who doesn't live particularly close to any flyable hills, this would mean I would save significant amounts of time by not travelling back and forth to the Peak District, and have more freedom in the air when I did.

This form of powered paragliding could open up new worlds that the free-flight cousin could only dream of.

Paraglider to paramotor transition

Since I had a paraglider wing already, I figured the additional investment required to transition to paramotoring would be relatively modest; all I would really need was the motor itself. I had the helmet, the boots, the wing, and so I looked into the cost of one of these paramotor units.

I was to be disappointed - they were more expensive than I had bargained for. It seemed for a new unit, the average cost across a series of different brands was somewhere from £4,000 to £5,000. There were some brands which were a little cheaper, and some which were more expensive, but generally this appeared to be the going rate. For what is little more than a lawnmower engine, a harness, a cage to stop the lines of your paraglider getting caught in the propeller, and the propeller itself, this still felt like a lot of money to me. However, as I had already paid out for the wing that was not delivering what I had really wanted, I thought the least I should do was contact a local instructor and go and check it out. It turns out that my local instructor was about a 20-minute drive away and also went by the name of Peter. For ease, I shall now refer to him as 'Peter2'. I called Peter2 and arranged to meet him from his field the next Saturday.

I turned up to Peter2's field, and the first benefit from being able to launch from a flat field, apart from the obvious advantage that nobody here appeared to be spending all of their day walking up hills, was that you could drive your car right onto the field itself. Sounds trivial, but I would learn this is a real benefit when unloading your car with wings and motors in the months to follow.

Peter2 was a rather diminutive guy, very friendly, and we instantly got chatting about my experience to date and some of the key differences between free flight paragliding and paramotoring. I am naturally interested in what he has to say, but can't stop my mind from repeatedly questioning whether he is big enough to run with an engine on his back. He mustn't be a hair's breadth over 5 foot in height and I feel certain I have eaten wider chocolate bars in my time. My mind catches up and it appears I must have missed something important he has just said.

"Erm, sorry what was that?" I ask.

"Trimmers. Your wing won't really work very well with a motor if you don't get a new set of trimmers," Peter2 informs me. He takes me to look at the riser arrangement on one of his wings, and to my dismay there is a whole 'other' section with adjustable clips and toggles that I have never seen on any paraglider wing from my time on the hills.

"Ah, right then. Bugger."

Peter2 can see I am a little crestfallen from this news; I had thought all paraglider wings were basically the same and could be used for free flight or under power. But not all is lost as Peter2 tells me that if I call up the supplier they should be able to provide some trimmers and he would help me fit them. Nothing too expensive he assures me, and regardless it doesn't stop me from spending the rest of the day there, showing off the ground handling skills I have amassed to date - which turns out to be rather trickier on a flat field than a hill, insofar as wind is not being pushed up the hill and instead comes from across the surrounding trees that line Peter2's field. Whenever wind is being blown over objects, trees or buildings for example, it becomes disturbed and is no longer smooth and predictable. This is generally referred to as 'rotor', and in such conditions paraglider wings are susceptible to flopping around which makes kiting the wing more challenging.

I meet one or two of the regulars; middle aged men who have been flying for a few years, a young chap called Dan who is starting out at paramotoring from scratch, and a young girl called Katie. Katie, it turns out, is the daughter of one of the regular guys and also flies a paramotor. Katie is 16 years of age, average build for any girl that age, and is able to throw one of these so called *heavy* paramotors on her back and take to the skies. I was beginning to rethink the rumours I had heard on the hill, whilst para-waiting, of just how heavy and cumbersome these units were.

One of the overwhelming impressions I had as I left the field that day, was the camaraderie between everyone there. It felt like a little family. Everyone was helping each other out when wings were getting folded over, sharing drinks when we stopped for a rest, joking around, yet when Peter2 took to the skies to give a little demo of a flight on a paramotor, we all stopped and cleared our stuff out of the way; giving him right of way for the field.

Watching someone launch a paramotor is a strange sight at first. The wing is kited in the way I was used to seeing on the hills, but then the pilot squeezes the throttle in his hand and the thrust from the propeller starts to push him along; his feet appearing to only barely keep up with the rate it is pushing him along, until the pilot is gradually lifted into the air, feet still running for a step or two like some cartoon character who has not realised the floor has been moved from under him.

The short flight however left a lasting impression on me. Peter2 was soaring around wherever he wanted, as high as he wanted, followed by some sharp 'wingovers' and then a low pass to give us all a wave. This was what flying was meant to be – unrestricted. Complete freedom to go wherever you wish.

I went home that evening with a rekindled passion for having found what I was looking for. I would phone the supplier of my existing wing in the morning and order one of these new trimmer sets.

Not all wings are created equal

Now I should, for those completely new to paraglider and paramotor wings, outline just a few brief points on the different types. Ultimately, they all do pretty much the same things, but some are more suited to different flying styles, and importantly the skill level of the pilot, than others. As a rule, speed and handling are exchanged for passive safety.

At one end of the spectrum there are *Beginner* wings, certified as 'EN-A' (different rating systems are used depending on the country you reside) which implies that they react very predictably in unstable situations; such as during a partial collapse or very thermic conditions. They will correct themselves for the most part with zero pilot input within a couple of seconds. The trade-off is speed, and how agile they move in the air.

This scale then moves through EN-B and EN-C to the highest rating of EN-D (intermediate through to advanced levels). An EN-D wing will be highly manoeuvrable and fast, but more susceptible to collapsing in rotor or rough air, and when they do, will generally require pilot input in order to correct. A collapse is not a one-way ticket to the Grim Reaper, but will naturally result in loss of altitude whilst the wing corrects itself and starts to fly again. There are some competition wings, used at the very top end of performance, which are unrated. Needless to say, if you have to ask yourself if you are ready for one of these advanced wings then the answer is 'no'.

The wing I had purchased off Peter1 was, as expected, an EN-A. It was a dedicated free flight wing and as such lacked these necessary 'trimmers' which, by altering the profile of the wing, could enable the wing to be better suited to higher speeds when power is applied.

After getting in touch with the supplier, I learnt that my particular model did not have optional trimmers; earlier models of the same wing did it seemed, but by a cruel twist of fate the model of wing I had did not. To say I was disappointed would have been an understatement. I had bought a wing for a couple of thousand pounds which now would not be suitable for use with a motor, and I couldn't see a way of affording a new one along with the additional cost of a motor also.

It was time to call Peter1, whom by this time I had not seen for a few weeks, to tell him that I was thinking of taking up paramotoring. I have never broken up with anyone over the phone before, and I never imagined I would be doing so to a 40-year-old bloke, but he took the news well. He was happy I had found what I was looking for and wished me the very best. We acknowledged it wasn't him, it was me.

Then I asked him the killer question; whether he would refund me my recently purchased wing. Unfortunately, he had stock of his own to sell, and couldn't afford to take back wings that had been used (albeit briefly). With hindsight, I completely see his point and don't blame him for not giving me my refund – it was my rash purchase, before I had fully concluded that free flight paragliding was for me, which had caused this. A couple of years down the line, and I have learnt to take full responsibility for my own actions, but at the time this was crushing news because this was my last hope.

Peter1 did try to suggest some online paragliding forums that I could try to sell it on, and generally I feel he was as helpful as he could be. To follow would be a couple of weeks trying to sell my free flight wing in the hope I could use the proceeds to fund a new, paramotor specific, wing. However, given that wings are ultimately aircrafts which a pilot is entrusting his life to, the second-hand paraglider market is not exactly a hotbed of activity. If you think cars depreciate in value the moment you drive them off the forecourt, try paraglider wings that have been let out of their original bag!

So predictably, as ever when fools rush in; I was left with a redundant wing that I couldn't shift. I had resolved to continuing the training with Peter2, using his paramotor-specific wings, and kept practising my ground handling. I had made a mistake by being too hasty with my purchases, and so I committed to completing the training with

Peter2. I wouldn't buy any equipment until I had completed the training, and could then make an informed decision that this was for me. The training itself represented a rather small cost compared to the overall scale of the investment needed for the equipment, and so I went back into 'saving' mode with my personal finances, in order to be ready should I decide to purchase a new wing and paramotor. Only this time *after* my training.

Practice makes perfect

Peter2 had a very different teaching style to Peter1. Both were official instructors with their respective governing bodies or associations. Their varied style was, I believe, no indication of the associations themselves; from what I have seen the syllabuses are basically the same (later in the book I outline some of the associations in question, and provide some guidance on what to look for). It was the individual personalities involved that made the difference.

Whenever we were para-waiting on the hills with Peter1, he would be taking the opportunity to talk theory. Weather patterns, QFE's, airspace were all regularly discussed in just my short time with him. By contrast Peter2 had a noticeable 'hands off' approach, which I confess, I found a little off-putting at first. Having come from an environment where it seemed no time was wasted, this style of training was more a case of 'learn through repetition'. And the repetition in question was ground handling. Once I had proved I could control the wing then I could move on to using the motor. Soon after that would be a tandem flight with Peter2 at the controls, and thereafter my first solo flight.

For any budding pilot's reading this, let me be quite clear. *Ground handling is the absolute worst part of the journey*. Watching someone experienced at the reigns only made it worse. Why could they get the wing directly over their head with what appeared to be minimal inputs? No jumping around underneath. No sweating as they chased the wing around the field. They could plant their feet, and with a light pull on the risers the wing would be over their head; sat there apparently waiting to fly.

When I attempted the same thing, the wing would come up asymmetrically, a pull on the brake handle later, and the wing would be end-over-end. In the brief instances when the wing was centred over my head, the wind would die just a little and the wing would fall.

Even now, years later, when genuinely I don't recall the last time I failed a launch, I still find it very difficult to explain what it was I found so difficult. It isn't one of those skills that simply 'clicks' in a moment of golden realisation, but for me at least, was forged slowly over months and months of hard work.

Given I was working five days a week, and the weather in England is not always conducive to guarantee two solid days of practice at the weekend, I was perhaps averaging a day's training every two weeks. Those are long intervals between sessions when you are trying to embed a new skill set.

I recall very vividly, maybe two or three months after first meeting Peter2, that I was still unable to control the wing over my head for long enough to satisfy him that I was ready to progress. After another wing collapse, I completely lost my temper, fell to my knees and started to hit my fists into the ground. Not my finest moment I'll admit, but I had been training now for around 6 months if you counted my hill experience, and I had yet to get a proper flight under my belt. I felt thoroughly frustrated.

The big drawback with training with a motor was there wasn't really any opportunity to do short flights. You were either ready to fly with a motor or you weren't. There was no opportunity to go for little hops down a gentle slope, just to scratch the itch and confirm your efforts are going towards something.

It was then that one of the regulars, John, who was down the field on the same day, came over and offered to watch what I was doing. I picked myself up and started to kite the wing once more; struggling with the inconsistent wind and rotor from the trees. It fell back down to the ground after maybe 10 seconds and he patiently shook his head and said "No, no, no. Make love to it; don't fuck it!"

I'm sure you will agree John had the heart of a poet.

Over-correcting appeared to be a large part of my problem. There is a subtle finesse to feeling a wing interact with the wind around it, and manipulating this to gain control is a skill I was not given at birth. When the wing was going left, I was pulling too hard on the brake line to bring it back in line and instead going too far the other way. This was then leading me to pull the other brake line and you quickly descend into a mess of trying to correct your own prior corrections. My inputs were just too big; a gentler but firmer touch was required.

I owe it not only to my instructors, but all the other people who have helped me with little bits of advice as I progressed, and continue to progress to this day. Maybe it is because flying is such a minority sport that all the people who partake are so generous with their time and knowledge. Everyone I have met is happy to help, eager to share their passion with like-minded others. If you follow me into this sport I am sure you will discover the same character traits in those you find.

Further progression and tandem flight

Not long after, my skills at wing control had reached a level where Peter2 started to introduce the motor. Not with the engine running or the propeller spinning, not just yet; for now the challenge was kiting the wing with the added weight of the motor on your back.

There's no getting around the fact that the added weight feels like a hindrance at first. Different brands of paramotor vary, but a 'dry' paramotor (i.e. without fuel) can range from between 20kg to 30kg on average. Then there's the added weight of any fuel (most have fuel tanks of maximum capacity around 10-14 litres) so the weight of the fuel itself is not to be overlooked. It is because of this reason that very rarely will a pilot completely fill his fuel tank; carrying fuel you are not planning on needing is simply excess weight making each launch that little bit trickier, your fuel consumption in the air that little but less efficient, and your landings that little bit faster. All in all, it was the equivalent of carrying a small woman on your back.

It is at this stage that you feel like you are starting all over again. The excess weight of a motor on my back tired me out faster, as you would expect, but just when I was starting to get to grips with this new challenge - next comes the helmet. You might not think this could make a difference, but with your peripheral vision now restricted, the muted effect of the ear defenders, and the bulk of the helmet itself to contend with, you would be surprised at how much more challenging it is. After I could manage all of that, then gloves get added to the equation. Now all feeling of the controls in your hands become vague, the dexterity of your fingers reduced. And so it continues; each new addition making it just a little bit trickier. It is a case of one step back in order to take two steps forward. Time spent practising now was ever sharpening my technique so the real launches would be smoother.

I kept reminding myself that I had seen a 16-year-old girl fly a paramotor. If my descriptions of the additional weight on your back and the exhaustion it can create when you are ground handling has put you off; don't let it. When you are preparing to launch for real, the amount of time you stand around with the motor on your back is minimised. You clip in, pull the wing over your head, throttle on, and as soon as the wing lifts you from the ground it takes the weight of the motor also. A typical launch will take around 20 seconds; experienced pilots don't stand around with the weight of the motor on their backs. After the launch itself, flying a paramotor through the air is as effortless as sitting in a flying chair – the wing takes the load and you are left feeling unrestricted.

By now the date was early September, and the nights were starting to get darker. One evening after work I met Peter2 at his field for what I had been waiting for, and the final stage before my first solo flight; a tandem flight with Peter2 at the controls. I hadn't been in the air for months, since those short flights off the hills, and I was itching to taste some of the fruits of my labour.

Paramotors are generally single seater aircraft, but most instructors will have the appropriate equipment (harness, extra-large wing etc.) to take a passenger up for a flight. I would only recommend learning with an instructor that offers this service as part of their training – it really is required for a new starter to know that this is an activity they want to pursue. You wouldn't want to, like I did with free-flight paragliding, buy the equipment and invest your time only to learn that you don't enjoy the end experience for some reason. Most will offer this service as a one-off experience, for a rather nominal fee, without the training that goes along with it. It is a great introduction to the sport, and even if you don't take up paramotoring yourself, it will give you memories that will last a lifetime.

The setup of the tandem is such that, as the passenger, I was stood in front of Peter2 but we are both facing forwards. He meanwhile is wearing the motor on his back, with the throttle and brake handles in his hands, and we are connected together by a metal harness arrangement that isn't nearly as uncomfortable as it sounds. My helmet is on and my ear defenders down; I can hear Peter2's voice through the headset so we can communicate with each other. My only job is to run in a straight line – Peter2 will worry about the wing and throttle control. We both have our own harnesses so, once in the air, I can sit back and enjoy the view.

And what a view I was in for. You really don't need to fly very high, 500 feet or so, before the world falls away and nearby houses and cars start to look very small. Unless you live on a hilltop, or at the very least in wide open spaces, you can only really appreciate how large the sky is when you can see horizon to horizon. A further thing that struck me, having launched from a field not many miles away from one of the largest cities in the north west of England, was just how *green* the world is. In an area not known for its outstanding natural beauty, get a few hundred feet in the air and you can't help but be amazed at how fresh, lush even, the world appears. Farm land, tree lined avenues, playing field; this is the view the birds enjoy; the view of the God's even, and from up here the world looks bright, colourful and beautiful. Staggeringly beautiful.

Areas familiar to you suddenly look a little different. That curve in the road you never appreciated when driving along it; that lake you never knew existed; the large fields behind the houses which have horses running on them. The world looks familiar yet different all at the same time.

My reverie is interrupted suddenly by Peter2's voice popping into my ear asking me if I'm OK. I had forgotten he was there to be honest. I signal that I am fine, and he passes me the brake line controls. A further benefit of a tandem; getting a real go at controlling the wing in the air without the stress of launching and landing.

Here I discover another benefit to this type of aircraft; the ease of the controls. All my troubles on the ground seem to have evaporated now in the air. There is tension on the brake lines now we are in the air, so turning left for instance is as simple as gradually pulling the left handle down. The tension is gradual, so as you pull the handle down, you bank slightly and turn left. It's a very natural sensation – the danger of pulling too far and entering a spiral dive, which I had been pre-warned about in my training, seems utterly remote. Since you can feel the tension as you pull, you feel completely in control. You feel the dynamics so clearly that you toy with the idea of closing your eyes while turning; confident that you could still sense how far you are turning without the use of your sight.

Before I know it, Peter2 is asking for the controls back so he can prepare for the landing. I have no idea how long we have stayed in the air, but the memories are etched on my mind. Peter2 approaches the landing field, telling me to 'get out of the seat' of my harness ready to run, and we swoop in above the field and come to a gentle stop; placing our feet back down on the ground and jogging off the excess speed.

My girlfriend, Laura, who has been watching from the ground, runs over and hugs me. I feel like an absolute hero. Landing on your feet will do that for you. There is such a sense of satisfaction when you swoop down and land on your feet, and the best thing is this feeling hasn't left me even after a few hundred flights. Practicalities of not needing a runway put to one side for a moment; landing on my feet just as the super heroes of my childhood do remains one of the most pleasing elements from this type of aircraft.

I'm not sure I slept that night – I was too excited. That was the penultimate stage of my training completed. Only my first solo flight now remained.

First solo flight

There is nothing that really prepares you for that first flight. The fear, the excitement, the complete and utter mind blank...

I laid out my wing facing into what little wind there was. In light winds, this is critical to a successful launch, and I take my time to double check my lines are clear and all is ready. My heart is beating through my chest, and my hands are a little sweaty underneath my gloves. Most of the regulars are down the field also; someone's first launch is a rite of passage nobody wants to miss. Ordinarily you would expect a crowd to increase the anxiety, them watching for any little mistake that I might make, but I have spent so long with these people now and had so many struggles that they no longer feel like strangers. They are friends; there as support and wishing me well.

I go over the wing once more, checking the position, checking the wind sock; throwing some grass in the air to check the wind sock was telling me the truth. I was finally happy that the wing was in the right place and set up ready. Now to sort myself out. I am mentally rehearsing all of the little steps and techniques that I'd practised so hard for far too many months.

Peter2 steps back and speaks into his radio. Wearing ear-defenders the world becomes somewhat muted, but I can hear his voice in my headset clearly and confirm as such. The paramotor is on the ground in front of the wing and I crouch down and clip in. Peter2 walks over and offers me his hand to pull me up. The motor feels heavier than it did before, when I was only practising. The realism is setting in.

He reaches over my shoulder and pull starts the engine. The engine roars into life; I can feel the gentle vibrations through the harness and hear the sound of the propeller spinning behind me. A quick blip of the throttle that is strapped to my hand reminds me of the horsepower strapped to my back. I have felt this before when ground handling but this time is different; I'm going to use this little engine to take to the skies.

Peter2 steps back and asks through the radio "Ready?"

I think my knees might actually be shaking but this is the moment I have been waiting for. "Yep," I reply.

I take a deep breath, hold my arms out wide, and run forward. The tension on the lines pulls my arms back but I continue to move forward, each step getting easier as the wing is pulled from behind me to above my head. Peter2 is giving me the thumbs up and then his voice appears in my head urging me to "lean back and full power!" I squeeze the throttle in my hand as tight as it will go and the thrust from the motor suddenly takes over; pushing me along rather than me running ahead. I move my legs forward under me, preventing me from falling over face first as opposed to genuine running. I have lost all sensation of the wing above my head but it must be OK because Peter2's voice is repeating in my head, "full power, full power, full power..."

Just when I think my legs can't keep up with the speed that the motor is pushing me along, everything becomes smooth. My vision is no longer bouncing with my running, and I realise my feet can no longer feel the ground beneath me. The weight of the motor on my back disappears, being hoisted up behind me by the wing itself. I clear the trees which are enclosing the field and look down as I pass over them, looking at the tree tops between my feet. The feeling I experienced on my tandem flight, of the world falling away, presents itself again and the sky opens up. It's a beautiful sight, and I inhale the fresh air which is rushing at my face. I can hear wordless encouragement from my headset; Peter2 and the others in the background cheering and clapping.

After some moments have passed I realise that I have not yet lessened my grip on the throttle; I'm still squeezing the hell out of it. I slowly ease off and my altitude appears to level off. This is fantastic! But as my mind catches up with the sensory overload I have just subjected it to, I realise there's something wrong. The harness straps are digging into my inner thighs and it is beginning to hurt. I have not yet got properly into my seat.

I try to kick my legs up to cause myself to fall back into the seat but it doesn't seem to be working. I had previously done this on the ground during a 'hang test' but it doesn't seem to be working now with the engine running. The engine is half way up my back, and my arms are outstretched above my head with the brake handles in each hand. Lessons I have heard time and again in the field are replaying in my head – *"Don't pull both brakes down or you could stall the wing."* I look up trying to find the magnetic holds for the brake handles but can't find them. If I could hook up just one of the handles it would leave my hand free to grab the seat and hoist myself in. But I don't yet have the confidence to let go of a brake handle, and I start to panic as I can't locate the small magnetic holders.

Peter2 realises something is wrong and his voice booms through my helmet, "Are you OK?"

I press my radio button on the left side of my helmet, and shout back "Peter, I can't get in my seat!"

He stays calm at the other end, and repeats instructions to kick myself into the seat or to 'park' the brakes and grab the seat. I continue to kick my legs up but the seat isn't coming out from behind my back. Then Peter2's voice gives a new instruction, and becomes more urgent; "full throttle, full throttle - you are getting a little low."

I had been so busy trying to get into my seat that I had forgotten about my altitude. I was beginning to drop too low down, so I instantly squeeze the throttle which pushes me forward and upwards simultaneously. By now my legs are starting to feel a little numb from the tourniquet effect the harness straps are having across my upper thighs.

After I have gained more height again I can ease off the throttle and try once more, now with one of my hands free to assist as opposed to squeezing the throttle. However it seems useless. No amount of kicking my legs or grasping for the magnetic holds seems to be working, so I decide to come back down to the landing field.

"Peter, I am going to have to land!" I yell into the mouthpiece.

"OK. I'll guide you in," Peter2 calmly replies.

He tells me to ease off the throttle entirely, and begins to guide me back to the landing field. With all of my panicking and trying to get into my seat, I have completely lost the landing field. It's a very scary feeling, and easy to do at first before your sense of direction has become attuned to flying. From up here individual people are near impossible to see and every field looks the same. I have not had chance to set in my mind any landmarks to help guide me back. I tell myself that I can't be that far away because Peter2 can still see me from the ground.

Peter2's voice comes back on, "Gently pull on your right brake handle. That's it... a little more... right.

Now you should be able to see the field directly in front of you."

A wave of relief washes over me as I can indeed identify the field, and a few small dark spots against the green which must be Peter2 and the others. I continue to glide down towards the field.

Peter2's voice again. "You are into wind but a little too high, so we are going to put in some turns to help." He tells me to brake left, and I do so until the field is now on my right-hand side.

"Good. Now a right turn... that's it keep going." I put in the right turn until I am facing the other way, with the field now on my left. I have had this technique explained to me before – effectively weaving in a series of 'S' turn's - so you lose height but don't overshoot the landing field. A final 90 degree left turn and I am back facing the field but much lower now.

"I want you to kill the engine, and hold both brakes up high," Peter tells me. I press the kill-switch on top of the throttle and the engine dies. Now I am just a paraglider coming down over the trees of the field.

"I would usually tell you to get out of your seat now but I don't think we need that." He still has time to joke.

I'm focussing at the ground, which appears to be rushing up at me too fast. *Alarmingly fast*. I had been warned this can happen when you are not used to it

– the apparent speed that you come into land can be very disorientating until you get used to it.

Just as I think I am about to hit the ground with bone-breaking impact Peter2's voice comes back very clear and very loud. "Flare. Flare. Flare," he shouts and I immediately pull both brake handles from above my head to down at my sides. Instead of falling down, I level off. For what feels like a very long moment I am flying level once more – this time a couple of feet above the grass.

"Run. Run. Run." Peter2 shouts and I feel my right foot hit the ground. Before I know it, I have fallen forward; my left leg not being fast enough to continue what only with the upmost charity could be classed as a 'run'. I am face-first against the grass having sprawled out forwards, the additional mass of the motor having added to the momentum and speed, and it is on top of my back with the all-too familiar weight. I look forward from this vantage point and can see the wing fall in front of me. Suddenly the burden on my back is being lifted; John is helping me up and Peter2 is shaking my hand.

"Put it there, *pilot*," he generously dubs me. I am so full of adrenaline that the world is a blur; I don't feel much like a pilot, but I feel fantastic. I notice the warmth as blood begins to re-circulate back into my legs. I am being patted on the back, and there are smiles everywhere. I am hugging Laura and only then does it occur to me to check the paramotor over. I have just had a crash landing and it wasn't even my machine! Thankfully it is in one piece; by virtue of me having fallen forward I took most of the impact. I dust myself off and inspect the grass stains on my knees, but other than that I feel fine. The motor and I have survived.

Whilst Peter2 passes me a cup of coffee that he has been brewing out of the back of his van for just such an event, I am left with a pearl of wisdom from one of the regulars; "Every flight you walk away from was a good flight."

It was a short flight; indeed a rubbish flight by many standards. But in that short rubbish flight, I had amassed roughly ten times the amount of air-time that all my prior months spent on the hills had yielded. And this was a short flight; I don't think I had burnt more than half a litre of fuel. A flight where I could fly in whatever direction I wished, as high as I wished, and landed back in the same field I had taken off from.

True there were many lessons to be learnt from this, and thankfully they were quickly rectified. The brake magnets are not that difficult to find; once you can calmly assess the situation. I now fly with an additional foot stirrup attached to the seat which means I can hook my foot behind me to bring the seat underneath me. This is a very cheap and hugely helpful modification.

But overall the thrill of being your own pilot is immense. I had found that sense of *freedom* that I imagined personal flight should provide... I think I ordered my own wing and paramotor the next day.

Versatility of flight

Over the coming months I was flying every opportunity I got. Which, because we were entering Autumn, was not nearly as often I wanted. Daylight hours were on the decline, which was leaving me with any weekend day which was not wet or too windy.

A warning to all budding pilots out there: you may well become a little obsessed with weather watching. I have at least three different forecasting sources on my phone which I can check in a moment's notice. Unfortunately, paramotoring is heavily weather dependant, so planning a flight far in advance is uncertain, and the weather in my part of the world is unpredictable outside of a couple of days. If you happen to live in more temperate parts of the world then I am very enviable.

Wet weather is one aspect; rather easily forecastable and therefore avoidable. On a rainy day, most wouldn't want to be in the air anyway. Wind is the trickster, or *gusts*, to be more precise. A steady wind is predictable, whereas wind that picks up momentarily, to die down again, to only pick up again with no foreseeable pattern is potentially dangerous.

During flight, gusts are not an issue. You may temporarily feel a 'wobble' but most modern wings can absorb such gusts without any trouble at all. The danger is when on the ground but 'clipped in' to the wing – when preparing to launch for example and a gust takes the wing before it has had a chance to get overhead. On such instances you are liable to being dragged across the ground, if the gust is sufficiently strong, and this can be a very painful experience. These wings are typically 20 to 28 metres square, so offer a surface area which is clearly designed to be large enough to provide enough lift to fly. When this is laid out to the side of you – directly in line with any wind – then it can very easily pull you off your feet and across the ground. It has happened to most pilots, during their early years until they have a full appreciation for the weather conditions it is suitable to fly in.

Related to weather, and a point I should cover now, is the natural questions you may have regarding the time of year suitable for flying. There is no flying 'season'; any day of the year when weather is favourable will be fine. Contrary to initial perceptions, Winter is actually one of the better times of the year for flying. The temperature, or specifically change in temperature between day and night, is least pronounced during Winter and Summer, and these tend to result in the most stable air conditions. When there are more significant changes in temperatures, such as in Spring, then the conditions tend to be more thermic which can be off-putting or even dangerous for a novice paramotor pilot.

The obvious knock on effects of flying during the Winter months, without a cockpit, is clearly the cold. Even in the warm Summer months, if you fly to or above the clouds then the temperature drops notably. In the Winter, most pilots will wear a flying suit, a full-face visor (ski goggles work very well) and thicker gloves (again, ski gloves are perfect). Attired as such, flying with the air around you is just as comfortable as during milder weather. Don't let the thought of cold alone put you off flying as it can be easily managed.

Over the Winter, and into the next Spring, I took advantage of the more frequent flying occasions. It was during this time that I experimented with different *types* of flying.

Most aircraft can perform only one type of flying. The micro-light, which was my first introduction to the skies, travels within a relatively narrow speed range and, from what I have witnessed, always requires the pilot to actively hold on to the controls. A hot air balloon is brilliant for a calm, sedate journey across the landscape – assuming you want to travel in the direction the wind is going! The prospect of setting out and landing back in your own field, or intentionally stopping over at a specific destination, requires such favourable weather conditions that it can never be guaranteed. Helicopters, of all aircraft, definitely have access to a greater variety of flying styles than most. The ability to hover in a specific spot whilst getting that photo of your house, or landing in a specific spot, opens up more possibilities than most. As I will come on to explain, I have had a flight experience in a helicopter and it might not however be as great as it seems....

For now though I was experimenting with my new paramotor and the opportunities it can present.

Flying high? Sure. I have been over a mile high (5,280 feet) and know many pilots who have been up to 10,000 feet. To put that into some perspective, certainly in England, cloud base typically varies from between 3,000 and 4,000 feet – although the cloud tops themselves have the potential to be much higher. It will only be when you progress above 10,000 feet that oxygen starts to get lower, and for the avoidance of doubt the engine on your back will start to respond to the lack of oxygen well before the pilot will.

What about flying low? Flying low is where a paramotor absolutely shines. In what other aircraft can you fly so low, with such consistency, that you can drag your foot along the grass below you? Or across a river or lake, and feel that you are actually running on water? So long as you are obeying all the appropriate laws in your country of residence (I don't plan on discussing air law considering this book has a global audience and the respective laws will vary; but you won't be allowed to fly so low you can kick the chimney's off rooftops!) you will find endless fun flying around and interacting with the landscape.

Are they manoeuvrable? Definitely. Once in the air, wind direction is irrelevant, and they can turn so tightly that, should you wish, they can turn in an extremely small spot (say, a 5 metre radius). Dynamic changes in direction are very easy. Hovering is not possible however, and gaining height is restricted to any number of variables such as wing size and engine thrust, but I can be amongst the clouds after 10 minutes of launching should I wish. Losing height is very easy; ease off the throttle and you simply glide steadily downwards, and if that isn't fast enough you can put in some tight turns or 'wingovers' to aid the descent.

How about exciting, dare-devil stunt flying? Check. Being suspended under a paraglider wing ultimately means you are part of a system which acts like a pendulum. Meaning, at its most basic, that swinging is easy. The basics of acrobatic flight are available by using the very same equipment you need to float around the clouds; specific equipment is not a pre-requisite of acrobatic flying. There are specific 'acro' wings available but these are for the very advanced competition pilots; wingovers, spiral dives, up to the aforementioned 'infinity tumbling', are all possible on paramotors. High 'G' forces are very possible should you wish to get the adrenaline pumping.

What if I want to land in the field next to my friend's house? Assuming airspace laws are adhered to, sufficient space from buildings, people and other 'obstacles', and prior permission from the landowner, then this should be fine. Any reasonably flat ground will act as a landing field.

Ignoring the weather dependant nature of flying paramotors, which I have described already, *speed* is the one variable which cannot be greatly influenced. Now let me explain why that doesn't truly matter when you are flying for pleasure.

Speed is irrelevant

Speed is synonymous with fun, excitement, and danger. It is the key element in many 'extreme' sports, and in many of these cases, it is the sole constituent which makes it fun in the first place.

Driving a sports car wouldn't be any fun at all if the top speed was 10mph. Skiing would be a rather dull experience if you never exceeded walking pace, and downhill mountain biking would be very tedious in slow motion. With speed comes risk, and that can be the key ingredient for fun.

I would argue however that flying is not one of these occasions. Flying is fun not simply due to the speeds involved; which for paramotoring can seem rather tame considering the typical ground speed lies somewhere in the range of 20-35 mph - assuming no wind. If you are travelling into a head wind then this ground speed will reduce accordingly of course.

Flying anything above 1000 feet from the ground and the speed is very difficult to judge without the use of electronic instruments. It doesn't even seem like you are moving most of the time. This is simply a result of having no objects within close proximity which to assess your rate of progress – or to put it another way – if you are far away from everything, then it doesn't feel like you are moving even when you are. Only over a long period of time, or at great speeds, can progress be felt.

We have all felt this when being a passenger on a commercial aeroplane. Your typical 747 jumbo jet will cruise over 500 mph, but high above the clouds at cruising altitudes of between 30,000 - 40,000 feet, it doesn't feel fast at all. It certainly doesn't feel exciting; if you were on the ground and travelling at these speeds then the world would be a blur to your senses but at altitude I am often more concerned with the next in-flight movie I am going to watch. It is positively boring!

This then answers a question I sometimes get posed when I tell people the speed that paramotor's typically travel at; they say, "that doesn't sound very fast?"

I usually reply "No, it isn't. But that is missing the point."

Travelling at speed, such as commercial flights or on a high-speed train for example, is useful when all you care about is arriving at your destination; the simple act of getting from A to B. The aim in these instances is to of course minimise the amount of time it takes.

Flying for pleasure, such as what we have been dreaming about since childhood, is not about arriving at a destination. To quote an old cliché; *it is the journey, not the destination that counts.* Pleasure flights are about savouring the experiences, not rushing them. They are about the pure and simple joy of taking to the air, to relish the views, to discover new landscapes and have the humbling privilege of taking in the world from a unique perspective.

Travelling appreciable distances by paramotor is a challenge. A challenge some of us welcome, and I will discuss later the growing trend of 'adventure flying' or 'bivouac' trips; which is very much where I still would like to progress. For now I was revelling in my new-found freedom, sharing the experience with the new friends I had made, and experimenting with just what I could do with my new toy.

Set backs

"That was great fun!" I shouted over to Dan, whilst taking off my helmet.

Dan started to learn paramotoring around the same time as me, and we had both just landed having finished a flight together where we were flying low over the neighbouring empty fields. It was the early stages of Autumn now, and the leaves had just started to turn. We took the opportunity to fly low over the trees that lined the surrounding fields and thoroughly enjoy the vibrancy of the reds and golds that this season yields. Autumn is probably the rarest time of the year for good flyable days, as it tends to be quite windy in England, but this was a lovely still day.

We had been playing around for about an hour and decided to come back to the field for a drink. It was just the two of us as the rest were due to come down later in the evening. We planned to go back out for another flight, but this time in another direction as there were empty fields that we had yet to explore.

After finishing our drinks which we had stored away in our cars, Dan and I set up our wings for our second flight. We both launched fine, which having now spent the last year flying we had both amassed over 50 hours or so of flying time; failed launches or landings were becoming increasingly seldom.

The neighbouring fields, much like the one we trained and launched from, were lined with trees and hedges. On this second flight, in this new direction, I notice that the trees tended to be more spread out and I intended to try something I had seen online but never attempted before; tree slaloms. With a steady throttle, it is possible to fly at just the right height as to be skimming over the hedges but remain at the same height as the branches of the trees. With the wide spaces in between each tree, it is simple enough to fly down a line of trees and weave in and out of them. A paramotor is one of the only aircraft where such a thing is possible thanks to the relatively slow speeds yet great manoeuvrability they offer.

To put your mind at ease – such flying can be perfectly legal. There is a '500 foot flight rule', certainly in the UK but something similar will be in force in most countries, which states that you cannot fly within a 500 foot radius (imagine a bubble around you – so above and below not simply to your sides) of any building, person, other aircraft or general structure. If none of these things are present, like empty fields such as this, then flying below 500 feet from the ground is lawful. For the avoidance of doubt however, you must take responsibility to check the appropriate laws in your country of residence. Again, structured training would cover this.

The tree slaloms were a complete success. I was pleased to learn how precise you can be with the controls of the wing in order to perform this; steadily pulling left and then right on each brake handle to guide yourself through the gaps between the trees felt intuitive and natural.

I decided to head back to my landing field where I believed Dan had already landed. On my way back, I maintained the height I was travelling at – pretty much level with the tops of the trees. Perhaps it was the necessary calm following my earlier tree slaloms, a chance to relax now the stress of flying in such precise and risky conditions had past, but I was to make a very costly mistake which was due to my lack of attention.

I was approaching my landing field when I realised that I was too low, and should have been a little higher in order to clear the final trees which were lining the very field I was due to land in. I realised this too late, and instantly squeezed the throttle to gain as much height as I could and clear the trees. With instant full throttle, rather than smoothly gradual application, two things happen; firstly, the thrust pushes you along horizontally before the wing has a chance to generate more lift, and secondly you can experience a sharp 'torque steering' affect.

Torque steering is, due to the engine driving a propeller in only one direction (clockwise or anti-clockwise), the twisting force on the pilot as a result of air being pushed in that one direction. It is the scientific law of one action having an equal and opposite reaction; a propeller spinning anti-clockwise such as my motor effectively turns the pilot slightly to the right. This torque effect is happening all the time in the air, only it is very small it is hardly noticeable.

However, in this instance the torque effect of turning me slightly to the right was just enough to result in the very righthand tip of my wing coming in to touch with the branches of the large nearby oak tree. The next moments are still something of a blur as it happened so quickly. I recall being turned sharply to the right and down through the branches of the tree itself; each branch hitting the visor which thankfully was down over my face. The sole overriding thought, which I must put down to all the hours of training at the field, was *kill the engine*.

Whenever a launch didn't go correctly, and the wing would get twisted or start to fall behind me, *kill the engine* was the instruction which would sound through my helmet from Peter2. A failed launch could be embarrassing, frustrating even, but should the propeller continue to spin when the lines of the wing start to come down then it could easily suck the entire wing into the propeller where it would be effectively shredded. A couple of thousand pounds worth of gear could be down the drain in an instant, and most of the injuries sustained in this sport is actually from the propeller spinning whilst on the ground. The '*kill the engine*' command was one we all got used to hearing when training.

It was the only thought I had as I was tumbling down through those branches. I held my thumb over the kill switch on my throttle and the next thing I knew I was hitting the ground.

Doubts

My left foot was twisted below my body but other than that I'm on my knees at the very base of the tree trunk. By some lucky chance, the wing remained in the branches of the tree, with the lines from the wing effectively holding me and the motor up. I had landed on the ground, and my left foot had taken most of the impact, but the weight of the motor on my back was suspended just slightly from the ground. The propeller had stopped spinning so I guessed the engine had died before I hit the ground, but I couldn't tell if the propeller had been damaged with it still on my back.

Dan came running over and was asking me if I was OK. I was in complete shock but relieved to tell him I was OK; at worst it felt like I had twisted my left ankle. He helped me to unclip from the harness and wing, and moments after having a crash landing that could have been so much worse, I was lifting my motor away from the tree and placing it where I should have landed – on the field.

My wing however was less willing to join me, being draped across half of the tree. Me and Dan were trying to pull it down, but it was caught in a hundred different branches and it seemed impossible without ripping it out of there completely.

The aching in my left foot was getting worse, so I sat down on the grass and phoned Peter2. He, along with some of the regular guys, came down to the field almost immediately. They brought with them a large set of ladders and were able to get the wing out of the tree – but not without damage. An entire section of the fabric canopy had ripped – right down the centre – and I thought having seen this that it was a complete write off. To my amazement Peter2 and John both told me that damage like this was perfectly repairable! I looked at the shredded remnants of the wing and had serious doubts, but they passed on to me the name of a company to send it to and they would assess whether it was repairable – both Peter2 and John maintained their resolute opinions that it was nothing to worry about.

In fairness by this time I wasn't worried about the wing at all. Whilst this had all happened I was starting to doubt the pain in my foot was simply a twisted ankle. I could barely put any weight on it. It had been maybe an hour now since the fall, and now the adrenaline had subsided, the pain was deep and acute. I had called Laura when I called Peter2 and she had arrived not soon after. She decided almost immediately that she wanted to drive me to A&E at the nearby hospital to get it checked out, and by this stage the pain was bad enough that I didn't put up too much of a fight.

Accident and Emergency rooms are very unusual places. I hope that you never need go, but if you do you will be greeted by a very sobering sight. This was Saturday afternoon, and I ignorantly assumed that the place would be next to empty; the deep breath before the Saturday night plunge, for what most would expect to be a maelstrom of drink or drug related incidents.

It turns out that Saturday afternoon, and what I would now expect to be pretty much any time or day, is just as much a circus as the early hours of the weekend. It appears that many more people are having accidents, fights, and generally sustaining injuries than you would expect. The A&E room was littered with police officers chaperoning those that had clearly been in a fight, people being stretchered in with wounds to their heads, all waiting alongside those which had not the slightest outward signs of injury.

By now I couldn't walk at all, and my humiliation was completed through the need of a wheelchair as we went to register our case with a nurse who appeared to have spent a lifetime sucking lemons. A nurse which, from behind safety glass and with an air of regal indifference, took the very briefest of details and then handed us a ticket – I am not sure this was a raffle I wanted to win. I cannot articulate the shame of being wheeled up to a nurse and having to explain that I had flown into a tree. Credit it to her, she didn't even supress a snigger, but then perhaps in her line of work this was not the most ridiculous thing she had ever heard. It was however, the most ridiculous thing I had ever had to say to someone.

Around three hours, and several different nurses later, and there was the x-ray evidence hanging on an illuminated panel in front of me; I had broken three different bones in my foot. One in two different locations. Usually when life grants me the rare opportunities to look at x-rays, such as at the dentist, I have great difficulty deciphering what the blurry grey images are showing me. Not this time though - the glowing white x-ray of my bones had clear separation where even the medically untrained eye would not expect.

After having my foot and lower leg placed in a cast, I was introduced to a huge black plastic 'boot' that I would have to wear for the coming weeks. This boot came up to just below my knee, which seemed rather unnecessary given the damage was to my foot, but curiously enough it left my toes completely exposed. I still haven't figured out the rationale for this odd humiliation. Clearly it was designed by someone with a sense of humour.

Shortly after, and I was back at home. Since the fall, throughout the remainder of the day that was spent at the hospital, I had been secretly wishing that I hadn't been so complacent when flying so low. *If only I could turn back the clock. If only I had realised I was too low a little earlier.* All of these useless wishes circled around in my mind; none of which could alter what had happened. Now however, back at home, I was dwelling on what might have happened had I not been so very fortunate. I was starting to think about the future rather than the past.

I say fortunate because had the wing not caught at the top of the tree, at just the right height, then I could so easily have taken the full impact on the ground myself. I was rather protected from the weight of the motor on my back as the lines of the wing suspended it above the ground. Crashing into the ground with 25kg of metal on my back could have broken more than just the metatarsals in my foot. Had the propeller not stopped by the time of impact then it could have shattered and, still spinning, would have been thrown out in all directions and hurt either myself or any bystanders. Sustaining life changing injuries was very possible from an accident such as this, and thankfully narrowly avoided through nothing more than blind luck.

What would my life have been like if events didn't go exactly as they did? What would the future hold for me, and for the rest of my family? What guilt would I carry if I had injured someone else?

With broken bones, a broken wing, and feeling as low as I had in a long time, I remember asking Laura, "Do you think I should quit?"

It is when you are facing adversity that you find out your underlying character. Or indeed, someone else's character.

"No," she replied quickly. "You've just had a set-back, and that is no reason to quit. If you quit, you will always regret it."

The instant she said this I felt a great deal of relief. I didn't really want to quit, but I had been feeling guilty for putting her through the stress of almost watching me kill myself in the pursuit of a hobby. At the end of the day that was all it was of course; a hobby. A pastime. A sport. A dream that little children have which was a commitment both in time and money. Now that we had seen how easily it could have all gone wrong due to a momentary lapse in concentration I wouldn't have blamed her for asking me to quit.

And I will be forever grateful that she never has.

Risk and risk perception

Now, years later, I can look at the situation with more objectivity. I would guess that most people, when seriously hurt by an unnecessary hobby, would take the decision to no longer put themselves in harm's way. This would be a natural response that few would argue with. Why would you? Why take such risks for a brief thrill?

I have often been asked about the risks associated with paramotoring. There can only be one true answer, without false bravado or complacency:

Every time a human being takes to the skies there are risks.

Mankind, despite our seemingly inherent desires to fly which I mused on in the very introduction to this book, does not naturally belong in the air. Therefore, when responding to friends, family members or work colleagues when this inevitable question arises, I cannot with good faith pretend risks are not present.

I would however like to take some time to explore your own perceptions of risk. If, for example, my journey so far has potentially inspired you to follow your dreams likewise, and the very reason why you are even now rationalising away the possibility is due to risk, then I would like to challenge those misconceptions.

Risk is everywhere. There you go; a flippant, throw-away comment which we have all heard before. Everyone knows that risks are present in our lives, whether we choose to seek them out or not. But if you take the time to look at the everyday risks we blindly welcome into our lives, the risks associated with flight will seem trivial.

An obvious comparison is travelling by car. Transport of any kind introduces some element of risk due to speed and the chance of hitting either someone or something else. Most of us get into our car every day and travel miles, sometimes on motorways and highways at great speed, in all weather conditions, and think nothing of it. When was the last time you checked your tire pressures? Changed your oil? What about more mechanical issues that never cross our minds – how worn are your brake pads? For the most part, we rely on the diligence of others when taking our cars for an annual service. Let's all just hope that the garage does a good job and that an annual check will suffice.

Then of course there's the larger probability that it won't be a mechanical failure but a human one. You are travelling at speed, observing the rules of the road, and someone else crosses into your lane and crashes into you. Or they drive out at a junction without looking and go into the side of your vehicle. The risks are multiplied significantly when everyone is forced to share a relatively narrow strip of tarmac.

Any momentary lapse in concentration, and you could have a fatality on your hands.

Yet we all accept these risks every day because it is the 'norm'. It is average, even expected, for an adult to drive a car, and as such to introduce these risks into their life without a second thought. The real danger is that everyday risks such as this are taken for granted.

By contrast, every flight should begin with a pre-flight check. This doesn't have to be a huge burden, a thorough ten minute check of the motor itself, the propeller, checking that your helmet is clipped on properly, that the wing and its risers and lines are all as they should be. Not an annual check, done by someone else who you hope is paying attention. A check done by you, right before you entrust your safety to the equipment involved. Do you think you would pay thorough attention to this better than a mechanic who is servicing his tenth car of the day?

Again, to make the comparison, the consequences of a momentary lapse in concentration whilst flying is, more than likely, zero. Imagine you are busy flying over your house and trying to take a picture; you are not giving 100% focus on your altitude or the immediate airspace around you. In all likelihood the worst that is going to happen is you will change your bearing ever so slightly whilst leaning over to get that photo. The chances of hitting another aircraft? Next to nil. You are surrounded by free space; above, below and all around you. You will be like this the majority of the time you are flying – to see another aircraft in even remotely the same surrounding airspace is rare and actually a novelty.

If you asses these risks rationally, which activity - driving a car or flying an aircraft - seems the riskier to you?

But what about the altitude itself? What about an engine failure at 1000 feet up? This will change depending on the aircraft in question, but I happen to have experienced this personally whilst flying my paramotor, and the consequence is simply to glide back down to earth. A paramotor with an engine failure instantly becomes a free flight paraglider; the wing still flies. Unless this happens at very low altitudes, you should have a sufficient glide radius to make it to a suitable landing field – and if not then you are probably flying somewhere you shouldn't (say over a large body of water for example).

What about comparisons to other aircraft? I am assuming most of you have been a passenger in a commercial aeroplane? In any of these instances did you even meet the pilot? The co-pilot perhaps? Any member of the crew who wasn't simply dishing out lacklustre in-flight meals? That seems like an incredible risk to me – but one we all gladly take on a regular basis. Most of us have willingly placed our lives directly into the hands of people we have never met; happily committing our fates and the fates of those we love to faceless individuals.

When *you* are the pilot, *you* can decide when to fly. In what weather conditions? At what time of day?

With others or separately? Using what equipment? You are the boss, and with that comes the responsibility that you are going to minimise your own risks – not leave it to others to decide those risks for you.

A common law of financial theory, when making investments for example, is simply that *risk should be proportional with reward*. The two should, theoretically, go hand-in-hand. If you are only going to invest in a savings account, then you can expect the rate of return to be lower than if you were to invest that same money in shares of a listed company. The savings account return will be lower, but the perceived risk of the investment means your money is safer. Take less risk, and get lower reward.

The risks, and let me be clear that there are indeed risks, that I willingly introduce into my life from flying a paramotor are in exchange for a life-enriching pastime. This sport has given me so many great memories that the financial investment, the time I have spent ground handling down a field weekend after weekend, and the injuries I have sustained, are any easy trade in my eyes. I would do it all over again in a heartbeat. It remains, outside of the personal relationships I have enjoyed during my life, one of my very best decisions.

Acknowledge the risks. Acknowledge also that you can mitigate many of these risks before you even get into the air, and the ratio of risk / reward will balance firmly in your favour.

Coming back

After five weeks, I was able to walk back into the hospital and hand back my large, plastic, Robo-Cop-style boot. That was a satisfying moment, not least of which because I had been downing about 4 pints of skimmed milk each day in the attempt to reduce the doctor's assessment that my bones would take "between six to eight weeks to heal."

"Yeah, but you would tell that to an old woman who eats soup for dinner." This was my initial response to the doctor when he told me the timescales. "What about an active guy in his late twenties who is prepared to eat a protein-rich diet and drink nothing but milk?"

It's fair to say that I am not patient at being a patient.

After the doctor politely stood by his initial prognosis, I was determined to beat their estimates. I may well have been a little arrogant about the situation, but it frustrates me when medical professionals simply regurgitate something they learnt from a textbook without applying it to the specific individual. If I was an 80-year-old man, I would have been told "six to eight weeks." An obese teenager; "six to eight weeks."

Well I managed it in five. It is not my intention here to outline my diet or routine for healing quicker than expected. Being candid, I will never know if it was down to my diet or whether it would have healed at the same rate regardless. Like most people of my generation in today's world, an active lifestyle across various sports and gym memberships is not unusual. Most people who have spent even ten minutes in a gym environment will have heard the old adage *"you can't out-train a bad diet"*, and it was this basic thinking that fuelled my response.

I spent those five weeks eating lean protein sources, getting as much sleep as I could with a foot strapped up in that awful boot, and drinking nothing but milk. It strikes me as fundamental that if you give your body the nutrients it needs to build and repair muscle, ligaments and bone, then it has got to help the healing process. I was lucky insofar as I could work from home for the early part of that healing process, but after a couple of weeks I was back in the office and bringing in 3 Tupperware's each day of food, along with a 4-pinter of milk. I got some strange looks but mostly that was from having a boot that even an astronaut would describe as 'bulky'. Fortunately my close colleagues, clearly overwhelmed for my safety and wellbeing, never missed a chance to bring up the subject of those pesky trees which just jump out at you. They still remind me of this to this day... luckily I am not haunted by this harrowing experience!

In the meantime, the glider repair company managed to bring my wing back to health. In fact, this is a woeful understatement – you wouldn't have known this wing had been in an accident at all. I got it back a few weeks afterwards and it looked brand new. A week or so earlier, they discussed my options over the phone after they had received it and performed an initial inspection. They could ultimately do two things: a partial repair which would make the wing perfectly safe albeit the wing would be left with visible 'scars', or fully replace the entire section of the wing that was damaged. I chose the latter, and I was shocked with just how perfect it looked. They could even match the exact colour shade of the wing along with the stitching – in an industry where there are numerous different manufacturers of paraglider wings this is no mean feat.

Given the relatively modest fees they charged for this service, it amazes me just how they can manage it. It may also be worth noting for any budding pilot's out there; beware buying second-hand wings because any evidence of large scale damage can be easily erased. The company that fixed my wing did a very professional job, and I have been flying the same wing ever since which is a credit to their craftmanship.

Oh, and the damage to the motor? Nothing. Absolutely nothing. Not a chipped propeller, not a snapped cage line... nothing. My motor consists of titanium and carbon fibre mostly, and even though my foot had taken the brunt of the impact, I was nevertheless pleasantly surprised to see that there was no damage to my motor in any way.

So after a few months filled with drinking milk and walking like Robo-Cop, I was back in the field, clipped in, and ready to launch. I was more nervous this time than when I had my first solo flight! Back then I was worried about the technicalities of flight control, about technique and basic safety. Now I could launch, fly and land blindfolded (so long as no trees were in the way!), but overcoming the fear was the greatest hurdle. The fear of willingly placing yourself in harm's way to satisfy a dream.

But this was what all those months of slow healing had been about. I had been positively itching to get back into the air. I wanted to prove to myself more than anyone else that I could do it again.

Needless to say, I went for a high flight!

Going it alone

Not long after my first flight back and Laura and I are telling our gliding buddies that we won't be seeing much of them anymore. We had been looking for a new place to live during the last few months (some of the early viewings Laura had to go alone because I was still in my boot!) and we had found our dream house around 30 miles away. I love flying, but a 60-mile round trip every time I wanted to get in the air is too much even for me. As a result, I couldn't realistically continue to fly from Peter2's field.

Whilst we were in the process of moving home, I had been doing some research online to find any paramotor pilots in and around the new area we would be moving to. Peter2 didn't know of anyone around that area, so I was left to doing my own research.

Any budding pilots out there should consider finding your local group of enthusiasts. Typically the school you train with will provide an ongoing 'club', but this isn't just something that you will need as a trainee. It is one of the fundamental safety principles of any flight – *don't fly alone*. Forget the friendships and camaraderie for a moment, the true reason you shouldn't fly alone is safety. I have already explained my own accident whilst flying, and it was so much easier because Dan was there in the first instance able to help me. Had my accident not occurred on the very edge of our training field, Dan would have noticed that I hadn't come back and gone out looking for me. Had the incident been worse, I might not have had the opportunity to call anyone for help. Having people there who know you are flying and can expect you back is potentially lifesaving.

My initial research led me to a micro-light school which was very close to where I would be moving to. This was the same kind of micro-light with which I had my very first taste of flight, back as an early teenager. They didn't mention anything about paramotoring on their website but it seemed the best place to start.

I headed down to their airstrip one Saturday and introduced myself to the Chief Flying Instructor (CFI). This airstrip was slightly more 'developed' than the empty field I had been used to with Peter2; the grass was clearly very well maintained and it had large, corrugated steel barn-like hangars which stored the micro-lights when not in use. The CFI was a friendly enough chap, he had a couple of students with him at the time, and we had a coffee in his cabin (complete with sofa, small kitchen area and toilets – an absolute luxury considering I was used to an empty field!).

I explained that I was new to the area and looking for somewhere to fly from. I made it quite clear that I wasn't interested in teaching, and that there was only me - I wasn't going to invite a load of 'my gang' down to invade his field which I fully appreciated was how he made a living. Throughout the conversation I got the distinct impression that he wasn't really interested in having me use his field – I could use it but would have to give way to any micro-light that was in the vicinity (read: second class citizen), I would have to pay the same level of fees as everyone else to keep things fair (despite not needed a hanger to keep my equipment in!), and I would have to promise not to encourage anyone towards paramotoring. The last point I totally understand; teaching others was this man's livelihood and I was not at all interested in taking any business away from him.

Throughout all of this one of his students, whom I assume was still in the early stages of his micro-light career, was asking me several questions about paramotors as he clearly did not know what they were.

"So, they can be folded up and fit in the boot of your car?" He asks as he is looking at my rather small two-seater coupe.

"Err, yeah that's right," I nervously respond, not wishing to lie to someone outright but nonetheless acutely aware out of my peripheral vision of the CFI raising an eyebrow.

But the student didn't seem to recognise the change in atmosphere as he continued with his enquiries. "And you don't need any licence to fly it?"

"Well no. As it is foot-launched it benefits from being largely de-regulated…" I let the comment die in the air rather than continue, although I think I can actually hear the mental arithmetic from the student's brain as he tries to calculate how much money he could save.

By now the CFI is scrambling around in his phone trying to find me the number of 'some farmer' who he knows allows paramotor pilots to use his land. He eventually finds the name and number. I can see the details on his phone, although I'm not convinced at this stage that this isn't some random contact of his that he is passing on in an attempt to get rid of me.

He passes the details to me and then explains that he should really take his student up for his next lesson. The student by now is counting his fingers and has made it onto his second hand. I thank the CFI for his time and we shake hands amiably. I wish the student the best of luck with his lessons.

All in all, it was the politest 'fuck off' I have ever received.

Flying buddies

Most of us don't have our own fields to fly from. Even the largest back garden will need to be clear of surrounding trees (as we have explored already they do have a nasty habit of jumping out on you) and other obstacles such as power lines. Assuming also that you are not related to a farmer, this does mean that eventually you will have to knock on someone's door, explain that you want to use their land for something called 'paramotoring', all the while stressing that it won't damage their crops and maybe we could come to a mutually agreeable price for rent of the land. Typically they won't have heard of paramotoring, so you will have to describe the act of strapping a petrol-powered fan to your back and taking off under a kite, but if you keep bringing the subject of price back into the conversation you should hold their attention long enough to get your point across.

It was while ringing the number I had been given by the micro-light CFI that I was rehearsing precisely how my own script for such a conversation should go. I had never done it before, having only ever flown from my instructor's field, but I had spotted some suitable farmland near to my new home. I held little hope that this number wasn't some random friend of the CFI who was about to disappoint me, but before I went out knocking on doors to random farmsteads I thought I should at least give the number a call.

Success! It turns out the number was genuine – maybe I wasn't going to need to go door to door after all. I spoke to the owner of the farm but he himself gave me the number of a guy called 'Danny' who was the pilot he had an existing agreement with. The farmer seemed very laidback about the whole thing, but it hinged on Danny's opinion; if Danny was happy for me to fly with them, then the farmer would be happy to let me use his land on the same basis.

I then called Danny and told him of my situation; that I had recently moved to a new house and was looking for some local pilots to fly with. He seemed very open to the idea of me joining them. He said there were a handful of paramotor pilots that fly regularly and that I should pop down to the field at the weekend and meet everyone.

I did just that. I was introduced to the new 'gang' which ranged from a couple of guys with several years of experience, right down to someone who was having his first tandem flight. It was great to see someone go through that experience for the first time, and brought back all of the memories of my own tandem flight; the nerves beforehand followed by the euphoria afterwards.

As I had found with the group I trained with, this new gang seemed just as close and supportive of each other. They were laying out one another's wings, the more experienced helping with pre-flight checks, and even I was given a role filming the tandem launch. I think there is something about flying, about facing risks in order to fulfil your dreams, that forges tight friendships very quickly. In the course of everyday life, at school or work for example, friendships take years to fully develop. It naturally takes a long time to get to know one another, to understand their character and humour, and to gel as a group.

What I have found in the flying community is a general *helpfulness* towards each other. Perhaps it is as simple as identifying the same character traits in others that we know to be within ourselves – a shared passion and nothing more. If that were true then fast, strong friendships such as this would crop up all over the place – in the gym, down the local dance hall, or football ground for example. I suspect that these environments don't have the same effect however. Do people really get to know each other in these surroundings and create, on some level, a sense of community and belonging? I am not convinced they do.

However I have a feeling that there is something specifically unifying about activities that involve greater degrees of risk or danger. There is some wondrous quality and respect for others that is created when the same dangers are shared. Competition and rivalry doesn't come into it. Nobody is trying to out-perform the rest, and instead this is replaced by an encouraging atmosphere. A genuine desire to see others succeed, and a shared sense of pride when they do.

The nourishing surroundings you experience in such circumstances can be very fulfilling, and I was very pleasantly surprised to find myself in such surroundings again.

Droning on

During the process of selling my first home, I invited three different estate agents around to value my property, before discussing further options for selling my house. It was a good opportunity for me to see, firsthand, the specialist skills that the profession employs; what in depth knowledge of the local market did each have? What marketing strategy would they use to best advertise my house?

I was to be disappointed on all fronts. It seems all that is needed to make potentially life changing decisions about the most valuable asset most people with ever own is access to the internet and the ability to read. I'm not even sure of that last point. Certainly, the expertise I was faced with amounted to looking at the historical sold prices of similar properties in the area and perhaps adding a bit more, because you know, I had troubled myself to clean the house beforehand. Or decorated the rooms in suitably neutral colours, or any other numerous not-in-any-way value adding aspects to which there is perceived benefit. One chap didn't even bother venturing upstairs before declaring his valuation. How about that?

Estate agents are, to my mind, the lowest form of life on the planet.

It was with great satisfaction that I eventually sold my house privately, foregoing their unsubstantiated fees, and as an aside to the intention of this book - but of altogether similar importance - I would urge you to do likewise. In a world of social media and camera phones it is genuinely baffling why people still feel the requirement for an estate agent to come around and try to 'sell' their house for them. Can't you take better pictures of your own house and post them online? Anyway, I digress...

It was whilst showing one of these charlatans around my residence, pointing out that the conservatory where he now stood was in fact an addition to the property that the local houses to which mine was being benchmarked were lacking, that he asked, "What is that?"

He had spotted my paramotor, sitting quietly in the corner of the room (I told you it was a small house) and so I explained what it was and, spotting his keen attentive mind struggling with the concept, showed him some pictures on my phone of me in flight.

"Oh, that looks good fun! It's a lot like my drone that I bought last year," he declared. It was my turn to look confused. "I bought it for work so we can take aerial photos of properties, but I use it a lot personally because I get to fly around and look at the neighbourhood and the views and stuff."

He then continued to explain how it "wasn't a toy", and generally sang the praises of his little remote controlled drone. Laura gripped my hand out of sight, sensing my growing incredulity and silently pleading for me not to descend into a rant. To my credit I didn't... so I thought I would do that here instead...

Even a mind as dim as an estate agent's must see the monumental differences between remotely controlling some small flying camera, and actually getting into the air yourself and flying around?

But it seems he is not alone. Drones have grown in popularity over the last few years to the extent that there is currently talk, in the UK at least, of introducing licensing requirements. The potential misuse of drones is a concern, and more than once they have blatantly floated into controlled airspace (like low level flying around an international airport!) and caused disruption.

The misuse of drones is one issue, but generally speaking, why on earth are people interested in drones in the first place? Yes, you can experience the views, and to some very limited extent enjoy the freedom that can bring, but are people really sitting around watching the world through a camera lens rather than getting out there themselves?

One potential argument is that there is no personal risk in flying drones. That is true, but there is also no *fun*. In the same way that strapping an action camera to a remote controlled car in no way replicates the fun of driving a fast car on a track, there is no genuine enjoyment from simply watching scenes unfold without actively living them yourself.

For our holiday this year, I am not going to waste money travelling in person to some far-flung exotic location. Instead, I am going to sit down and watch a 20 minute online video of any destination that springs to mind. Maybe I'll watch more than one. Maybe that will expand my horizons and I'll feel well travelled and a more complete human being for doing so. Maybe Laura will leave me and I will grow old, alone, glued to the images of beautiful locations and pretending I'm experiencing these things for myself. Or maybe not.

Perhaps you are a drone user? Perhaps you have considered purchasing one to get the sense of flight at no risk and a fraction of the cost? All sounds good on paper - but I would argue it is a fraction of the experience. Get out there and *live it*. All the fun is sat there waiting for you.

Noisy neighbour?

Despite flying from relatively remote farmer's fields, it is somewhat inevitable that people passing on nearby roads will spot you and come over to have a closer look. It is after all an unusual activity, and so at some time or another you will get an audience. Whenever people pull up near the field to watch we will always invite them in, and we have always found people are naturally curious about the sport and simply want to know a little more.

I recall one time when I was flying from my old training field and as I landed, a car pulled up next to the field. The field itself was rather tricky to find, was quite a distance from a main road, and the driver had clearly put in some effort to locate where I had landed. The car was full of students, 5 of them around twenty years old I would guess, and had followed my decent down because they "thought I had jumped out of a plane." They had spotted me around a mile off and traced the little back roads and country lanes in order to locate the field. Only when they saw up close that I had a motor strapped to my back did they realise I was not a skydiver and I spent 15 minutes or so chatting to them about paramotoring and answering all of their questions. It was great to see how enthusiastic they were about the sport and a couple of them were upfront enough to say they wanted to do something like this when they had the money to.

It is very much these sorts of people to whom I am writing this book. It struck me that most people are at the very least interested in paramotoring, even if they decide it isn't for them. Whenever I fly low enough to see that people are looking up at me or taking photos, I will always give them a little wave and, 99% of the time, they wave back. I flew over what appeared to be a class of young children at a local wood once and they all came running out towards me waving frantically. I gave them a little show by performing a couple of wingovers and they went crazy - jumping up and down and cheering. That put a huge smile on my face, and I hope that some of them find their way into the air for themselves later in their lives.

However, as with all things, there are some that don't see the good in life and instead favour a negative view of others having a little fun. In three years there have been two such instances of 'complaint' that I think would only be fair to share with you. It is worth you being very conscious that not everyone will welcome you flying, regardless of how far away from them you actually are.

The first happened just off the south coast of Devon after perhaps the first year of my flying career. I had gone down to Devon to spend some time with my Dad as I did most Summers, only this time I took my new paramotor equipment with me. Some of my family from my Dad's side were also down in Devon at the time, and most of these relatives live in

Canada, so this was a rare opportunity to show off my new hobby that they had heard about.

After much looking around, including once again being deflected away from a micro-light landing strip (I think they are jealous!), we were pointed in the direction of some flat coast line, next to a pub, right on the cliff edge of the sea. It looked perfect, and so I spoke to the landlord of the local pub to get his permission to fly from the site because I was mindful that this pub had an outdoor seating area and I didn't want to disturb his customers. He was a very friendly chap who quickly told us that paragliders sometimes fly from this sight and that it was no bother at all.

I set up and launched in the usual way, waving to my family on the ground that had come out to see what paramotoring was all about. I also noticed that all of the pub's customers who were seated outside were waving back, and there was more than one face at the pub's windows watching from the inside also.

It is always fun to fly in new locations, and gliding above the cliffs, where the waves came crashing on to the rock face, was great. The conditions were a little too windy to be honest, and I knew when I launched that this was going to be a short flight. I had been up perhaps 30 minutes and decided to fly back and land.

Upon landing (which I was grateful was a nice smooth landing in front of my family!) I was immediately approached by a young woman wearing a green uniform. She introduced herself and explained that she was working for the National Coast Guard and was acting upon a complaint she had just received from a local resident about the noise levels.

For those that have never visited Devon, imagine gentle rolling hillside and small little villages embedded within the valleys. There are of course towns and beachside locations, but your typical 'chocolate box' scene is not far removed from the majority of Devon. Where I was, being so close to the coast, was even more sparsely populated, with the odd little hamlet dotting the landscape but being miles away from the nearest village.

I looked around at the surrounding green hills confuscd, pointing to the pub and explaining that I had already asked the landlords' permission before flying. She suggested that the complaint, which she stressed was anonymous, had come from elsewhere. My initial reaction was to laugh. There was a single house that I could see perhaps a mile from where we were. I nodded towards the house and said "ah well, no prizes for guessing who then?" to which she, to her credit, appeared a little sheepish.

I went on to explain that I was never within 500 feet of the house, that the flight I had just done was in free air space, and I would be happy to upload the data from my GPS device to corroborate any of my claims. I probably came across a little stronger than I intended, having been challenged in front of my family immediately after landing, but I did stress that the flight that had just happened was entirely legal and the noise from what is basically a lawnmower engine is well below any legal 'noise pollution' levels.

I continued by saying "As it happens, I am only going to be flying from here for a single day as I am not local, but on behalf of my fellow paraglider pilots in the area, would you please feedback these facts to the member of the public who made the complaint," raising an eyebrow towards the lonely house on the distant hill.

In fairness, the young woman from the Coast Guard was very friendly and was only doing her job in acting upon the complaint. We both understood that, and by the end of the exchange she was actually asking me questions about my equipment and how my flight was! She seemed genuinely interested and I wouldn't be the least surprised if she was the sort of person who would ordinarily wave back to me when I fly overhead.

The second instance of public complaint was at my usual field, and differs to the first insofar as this complaint was made in person. I had just landed after a typical flight around my usual patch. It was a Summer's evening, around 7pm, and there were 4 of us flying, and since it was a lovely evening our families had also brought down some camping chairs and were sitting out enjoying the weather and generally having a good time.

A car pulled up by the roadside next to the field and a gentleman walked over and, with me having just landed, came over to speak to me. I thought it was the usual curious bystander which we got from time to time, and I was prepared to give my typical speech which I have entitled 'This is called a paramotor...'

Instead he leaned in close and asked, "Can we speak over here because I'm mindful that there are young children here and I don't want them to hear this?" Needless to say, I was somewhat taken aback, but walked out of earshot with him. He then began to vent his frustrations at having come home from a long day at work and had only just got his young daughter off to sleep, who was then awakened by the noise through her open window of my motor flying over the local village. Having some prior experience by now of a public complaint, I let him rant before attempting to respond.

He continued on about how he bought a house in the country for peace and quiet, he wasn't happy with us flying over the village, and why didn't we take off and fly in a different direction? I am pleased to say I responded very rationally, although I could so easily have pointed out the selfish flaws in this man's arguments; since when did living in the countryside grant a right to silence? When you bought your house how much did you pay for the airspace above it? Don't you think if we fly in the same direction all the time that this might have an impact on other neighbouring homes and villages in that direction? Wouldn't that be fundamentally selfish and unfair?

Some of these points I did gently highlight, to which he didn't have much in the way of answers. I expressed my sympathy with the difficulties of getting a young child off to sleep, but perhaps closing the open window is the simplest solution as opposed to hunting down any in the vicinity who have the cheek to live their own lives.

After explaining all of this to him, I suspect he felt rather foolish. Ignoring for a moment the more philosophical question of 'does a fool realise he is a fool'? We ended the conversation amicably; I promised to tell everyone who flew from this field that we should avoid flying over the village whenever possible, but that I couldn't promise that this would never happen or indeed that he would never hear the noise from our engines ever again... in fact I told him that this was inevitable. So for the most part we have an understanding, and we haven't seen him again despite flying regularly from the same field for over a year now.

How depressingly arrogant of these people who made their complaints; to feel that they own the countryside and can complain when others are enjoying it in a manner that displeases them. What challenging lives they must lead, when they feel a sense of ownership for what they haven't purchased, and their perceived right to impose their opinions on others.

Had I driven a Harley Davidson motorcycle down the winding country lanes, even right past their residence, the noise and 'disruption' would have been greater than me flying my little two-stroke engine 1000 feet above them, but would they have hunted me down to make a complaint? Would they have called the authorities to report my activity and demand that I be reprimanded?

I wish I could listen to how that conversation would go. "Officer, officer, someone is riding a motorcycle past my house and the noise has disturbed me. What are you going to do about it?"

Or perhaps to put it another way: "Someone is doing something I don't like and despite having no moral or legal right to say otherwise, I have such an inflated sense of my own self worth that I am going to kick up a stink about it." It's infantile at best.

The truth however, is that they wouldn't complain in these circumstances. The deep throttle-induced vibrations of a Harley Davidson whizzing past their house would have the picture frames rattling off their walls, and yet they wouldn't think to complain publically. And therein lies the problem that we as paramotor pilots face; *it is a minority sport*.

To some, a rare occurrence that causes the most minor disruption to their life is something to be stamped out - nip it in the bud, before it becomes socially acceptable. But a *common* occurrence that causes even more disruption is tolerated, accepted even. Had a plane flew over their house, at the altitudes that I was flying at (which would have been perfectly legal given it is free airspace) at most they would have remarked "that plane is flying a little low." Would they have phoned the Civil Aviation Authority to report this disturbance? Almost certainly not.

Most people are thoroughly welcoming and curious of paramotoring. There is a small minority that are not, and will try to 'nip it in the bud'. Smile politely to these people, explain that you are within your right to enjoy free airspace, and try to leave it on good terms. But most of all... secretly pity them.

Shake, rattle and hole

The innate challenge of any technology or tool, is not to become complacent with it. I assume, subconsciously, that when I close the door to the dishwasher that the cycle will run without issue. I assume that when driving my car that the wheels are not going to fall off, or that the lawnmower isn't going to fling its blade across the garden. Once we have used a tool for a couple of times, we take it for granted that it will continue to operate correctly for the next hundred times without fault; mostly we don't even think about it. It is of course inevitable that at some point the device in question will breakdown, but when this does we feel unfortunate and perhaps even shocked that this has happened to us.

However, in the world of piloting aircrafts, of any kind, you will be introduced to the concept of 'pre-flight checks'. When you are first introduced to this, if you are at all like me, you will be somewhat sceptical of the requirement to perform thorough pre-flight checks. I don't lift the bonnet of my car and check the oil level before each journey, or the air pressure in my tyres, or any other plethora of checks I could perform on my car. I trust that the car is in the same state in which I left it last. So why do I really need to perform pre-flight checks on my paramotor?

Some pre-flight checks make complete sense; principally because the situation or equipment has changed in some way since you last used it. A good example of this is making sure your paraglider lines are clear. What this basically means is ensuring the lines from the glider to the harness are in their proper order and not tangled in any way. Considering since you last used the wing, you will have packed it away in a stuff sack or concertina bag, wrapped the lines up and threw the lot in the back of your car, taken it all out again on the other side to store away, only to repeat the process in reverse ready for the next flight. This could easily provide the opportunity needed for the lines to get themselves tangled in some way. Laying the wing out again on the ground and checking the lines are clear before clipping in is natural and, frankly, doesn't take very long at all.

But the other checks that you are advised to perform... why do I really need to? After all, the last time I used it everything was fine so where are the devilish gremlins who, in the dark of night, are fraying my lines, or loosening the spark plug, or tearing the netting on my cage?

Now neither of my instructors ever suggested doing all of this before *every* flight, but certainly every couple of weeks or so (depending on how frequently you are flying of course) and whilst I listened dutifully as a student, nodding and smiling in all the right places, inside I was dismissing these checks are unnecessary. Once a year perhaps.

Before I tell you of a flight which changed my perspective on this, I would like to point out that I am only outlining this so you can learn from my mistakes. I have had hundreds of flights, the vast majority of them hugely successful, but telling you about each of those would be monotonous and repetitive. I am only outlining the 'bad' experiences so you don't make the same mistakes – please don't leave with the impression that flying a paramotor is dicing with death, because it really isn't.

The flight itself was much like any other. I had launched from Peter1's field and was going on a bit of a 'cross country' flight. Other members of the gang were on the ground, but I was the only pilot in the air at that point. I was heading back and decided to check my fuel level as to judge whether I had enough time for a little de-tour before landing, and was a little shocked to see that I didn't have much fuel left in the bottom of the tank; perhaps a litre or so. I probably put five litres in to begin with and simply assumed that I had been a little too heavy on the throttle, pushing against the wind for most of the flight perhaps, and used more than I had anticipated. This was no issue as I was not very far from the landing field at this stage anyway.

I landed without incident, and began to unclip and pack my wing up in the normal manner. It was only when I picked up my paramotor to lift it into the boot of my car that I noticed there was fuel leaking onto my shoes. I looked once again at the fuel tank and there was little more than a dribble left, but the leak was coming from a very small hole in the bottom of the fuel tank.

I should explain that the fuel tanks on paramotor's are made from transparent, reinforced plastic. They are very tough; you could stand on them and they wouldn't dint or deform, if you were to punch one you would only hurt your own knuckles. What then could have put this small hole in my fuel tank?

I hadn't noticed anything when breaking down my paramotor unit for transit. The cage was in one piece, and there were no clips missing or loose harness buckles. I checked over the propeller and did see a small dint in the carbon fibre on one of the edges. Then I spotted something missing from the cylinder head; the metal casing covered in cooling fins which encloses the underlying workings of the engine. It usually had four nuts holding the head in place. Only now there were only three, and a hole where the fourth should have been.

I can only surmise as to what had happened, but it seems pretty clear to me now the cause of the small hole in the fuel tank which, had I not been so close to the landing field, could have meant I would have ran out of fuel and needed to make an emergency landing. That could have ended quite differently if there was not a suitable place to land!

The vibrations from the engine, having been used for numerous flights before this point, had slowly loosened the nut from the cylinder head. This nut had finally unwound itself mid-flight, and fallen away and into the propeller spinning just inches from where it should have been securely housed. The propeller, despite being powered by a small single cylinder two-stroke engine, is still spinning at well over 8000 rpm at full throttle. The nut must have collided with the spinning propeller, and ricocheted off and hit the fuel tank. That is the only force strong enough to fire the nut at the tank with sufficient strength as to pierce a hole in it, and start what was a slow but gradual fuel leak. This would also account for the slight damage on the propeller.

When I think about it, I consider myself very lucky. There are so many ways in which this event could have gone slightly differently yet the outcome be much worse. What if, instead of the nut rebounding off the propeller into the tank, it alternatively went up into the wing? Or into my leg directly? The propeller is spinning around in circles so, in theory at least, the nut could have been fired off in any direction. Had it gone in the wing, would that then have created a tear which would result in me needing to throw my reserve parachute? What if I was not close enough to the landing field? What if I had only put in four litres of fuel and not five?

All of this because I didn't do thorough pre-flight checks and ensure that the nuts were adequately tight before taking off. Not a common check, and I won't pretend I check this now before every flight, but certainly something I am cognisant of now and for the future. This has also instilled good habits in terms of other checks which previously I would have dismissed out of hand.

There are so many little things that could go wrong, and the consequences from these faults could be severe. Don't be cavalier. Don't be complacent that just because something hasn't been touched since last time that it doesn't need checking occasionally.

Don't fall for the trick of assuming bad things only happen to other people.

Taste of a millionaire lifestyle?

When asked, I have always found it difficult to suggest gifts for myself. When a loved one asks about potential Christmas or Birthday presents, since leaving childhood, I have often found it a truly challenging question. It isn't that I don't desire things, but I certainly don't desire things that are less than £100 or so. I wouldn't have the cheek to ask for anything more expensive, and generally if I wanted something for less than £100 then I would have bought it for myself at some point rather than waiting for the next gift opportunity.

In recent years however I think I might have solved it. Experience days. There are numerous websites out there that offer experiences and over the years I have personally driven supercars (recommended), gone bungee jumping (the jump was good, but the hanging upside down afterwards as they lowered the crane was anything but fun), zip-lining (not bad), and for a taste of that millionaire lifestyle, a helicopter flying experience.

If I win the lottery tomorrow, or this book sells in its millions (the odds are probably similar), then I had always thought that one of the first purchases I would make, after a few beers no doubt, would be a helicopter. I have held the helicopter in high esteem for most of my life; envisaging the ease of transportation that only an aircraft which can hover, take off and land in relatively small areas, yet still travel great distances, can provide. What's more, given my passion for flying, I envisaged personally piloting the helicopter, taking all the necessary lessons and tests in order to attain my own Private Pilot's Licence (PPL) rather than simply being chauffeured around by someone else.

Oh yes, that would be a taste of the sweet life, and so I thought that for one of my experience-based gifts I would ask for a taster helicopter flying lesson, where I would take the controls for a short time to satisfy, albeit briefly, a long held yet unaffordable ambition.

After booking the experience, I turned up on a sunny Saturday to the local, small airport and signed in for my helicopter flying experience. After the usual form filling exercise regarding risks and liability, I was introduced to the young pilot who would be taking me for my lesson. He was, rather frustratingly, around my age; late twenties or early thirties perhaps. His name was Will, and he wasted no time in taking me over to the helicopter.

I was to fly a Robinson R22. Only a little two-seater, with most of the cockpit being enclosed by glass which, outside of paramotoring or something similar, offered a very good view to the pilot and passenger of their surroundings. I remember there was even a small glass panel on the floor by your feet, so you can see the ground directly below you, which was a nice touch.

Will explained some of the controls, and we start to discuss the flight plan for the 'lesson' (despite being purchased as a stand-alone 'experience', this half hour long flight could count towards the hours logged if I was to pursue a PPL, and so also counted as a lesson). He takes off, which even with ear defenders on under my helmet, as with paramotoring, was a noisy affair. Once in the air and stable he begins to demonstrate some of the controls in more detail.

Will talked me through 3 main controls. The first was right in front of me, called the 'cyclic'. It was not dissimilar to a joystick from an old gaming arcade, only it joined to a twin which sat in front of Will also. Effectively we both had a joystick in front of us, but they were joined in the middle lower down so, should I try anything too daring, Will could take control back off me. This seemed like the main control in terms of turning left or right, although it also moved forwards and backwards. I would be using my right hand to control the cyclic.

The second control was called the 'collective'. This looked just like a handbrake lever in a car, and was situated to the lower left of my seat so I would operate this with my left hand. This basically controlled your climb or descent, although I must confess I don't recall using this much in the lesson itself.

The third control, or controls, were at your feet. Two pedals, called 'anti-torque' pedals, which ultimately controlled the small rotor on the back tail of the helicopter but what effectively pointed the nose of the helicopter in the right direction. Pressing the right pedal would turn the nose to the right.

Like learning how to drive a car for the first time, the greatest difficulty is being placed in control of so many different things which often required simultaneous inputs. As a student driver, having to steer, control three pedals, change gear with the gear stick, keep an eye on numerous mirrors, as well as other things, can all feel like a little too much.

Well going from paramotoring to flying a helicopter was a little something like that. In paramotoring there are basically two controls; a throttle strapped to one of your hands which dictates your altitude, and a handle in each hand for directional control. Pull the left handle, and you turn left. What could be simpler?

In the helicopter, altering any one of the controls was simple enough, but trying to combine any two together made me feel like a learner driver all over again. But the worst part of it was the sensitivity of the instruments, particularly the cyclic.

When Will had first taken us up high, he asked me to put my right hand on the cyclic at my side and explained that he was going to let go of his side and then I would be in control of the aircraft. My aim seemed simple enough - to line up a small black line across the windscreen (assuming they are called windscreens in helicopters) with that of the horizon.

This would ensure that we were travelling straight and level.

"OK, you have control," he optimistically claimed as he let go of the cyclic from his side.

We almost instantly veered off to the right – not dangerously where Will would need to grab the controls back, but enough for me to need to concentrate to steady the small handle in front of me. I had moved the cyclic perhaps half an inch. *Half an inch.* That was all it took to move the helicopter a drastic amount and we had started to bank a right turn.

"Are you sure I have control?" I asked Will after I had steadied it and managed to line up the black line with the horizon. He laughed and said it was something I would get used to, but I couldn't help but ask "What happens if you sneeze when flying one of these?"

Half an inch is an incredibly small margin when you are not resting your right arm or elbow on anything in front of you. When driving a car, if you leave your hand on the wheel, most of the weight of your arm is going through the wheel itself and by extension, the steering column. The wheel is not so sensitive as to spin ludicrously from the weight of only your right hand at the side of the wheel, and for the most part you are able to rest your arm on something; an armrest or the door itself, to make even a several hour journey seem comfortable.

Try holding your arm out in front of you, a foot or so away from your face, and see how long you can hold it there before it starts to falter. Well I had half an hour of it to look forward to in my lesson. The issue magnifies also when you look away from the horizon or your hand, say, to look at the view or something whilst piloting the helicopter. When you are not actively concentrating on the horizon it is very easy to move your hand a fraction and suddenly be flying less than straight once again.

I had been used to doing most of my paramotor flying 'hands off'. Basically, after launching, I park the brake handles on their magnets and then I'm free. The flying is steady, I can steer using weight shift if I need to (literally just leaning in your seat), and with the throttle strapped to my hand I can almost forget about that also. For tight turns I use tip steering, and then I only grab for the brake handles when I am coming in to land and the final flare. Easy.

In fairness, I'm sure with more practice I would find a more comfortable manner to control the cyclic. The handbrake-like 'collective' and anti-torque pedals were less sensitive, and easier to intuitively feel, but I was left with the over-riding impression that flying a helicopter was not a completely relaxing experience. I find it difficult to imagine even a skilled pilot taking 5 minutes to get a camera out, set the focus, line up the shot, and take some photos of their house / a landscape / or whatever whilst remaining in control of a helicopter. This seemed like such a shame; taking the time to enjoy the view is one of the biggest benefits of flight.

During the flight I did use the opportunity to question Will on how he got into it, and of course the aspect that really interested me – how did he afford it? He naturally doesn't own the helicopter; he is an employee for the company that does, but I have looked into getting a helicopter licence and the cost of the lessons, tuition, exams, and logged hours needed for a PPL comes in at over £10k. This will vary depending on natural aptitude, but most of the cost is renting the helicopter and the fuel used to clock up the required number of hours – which is clearly pretty fixed. So that is £10,000 just to be able to legally fly a helicopter; not to own your own.

If you want to *earn* money as a pilot, then you need a Commercial Pilots Licence (CPL) and the estimate I was given was closer to £50k. The main difference is simply the number of logged hours required, as far as I was told. That's £50,000 of your own money invested in qualifying for a job, just like Will who was sat next to me. I was told these estimates by the firm who I had booked this experience with, and given Will was my age or thereabouts, and despite me having held a professional job since leaving college, I certainly couldn't entertain the idea of investing £50k of my own money to *maybe* get a job at the end of it. With my mortgage, I doubt anyone would lend me that sort of money.

Whilst we were flying, and he was effectively my temporary captive, I couldn't hold back my curiosity any longer. "Will, I know this is a rude question, but I have been told that the cost of holding a helicopter CPL is in the region of £50k, and I was wondering how you funded it. Did you find a sponsor of something?"

To his credit, he gave me a candid answer, "Well some get the experience they need through the armed forces, which is effectively sponsored I suppose. There are some who will get the backing of their families or parents if they are wealthy, but other than that most will take out debt in order to fund their training."

I didn't push for any details of how Will himself had managed it, but it is a rather bleak picture when you think about it. The main routes into piloting a helicopter as a career are basically to take out a potentially crippling amount of debt which you will be burdened with for years to come, get lucky and be born into a wealthy family, or pledge yourself to the Air Force for several years - which does come somewhat with additional commitments well above learning how to become a pilot!

During the flight, I asked Will about the helicopter's sensitivity to thermals (not much apparently) and other questions which must have given me away because he looked at me sideways and asked me if I was a pilot. I explained that I fly paramotors and surprisingly he said he always wanted a go at flying one of those. How ironic, that I had always wanted to fly a helicopter and instead was flying paramotors, and here was a man who flew helicopters for a living whom himself wanted to try paramotors.

He also mentioned something I had heard before; that quite a lot of commercial aeroplane pilots fly helicopters in their spare time. Apparently, the large 747's that we all use to go on our holidays every year almost fly themselves. I can't pretend to know if this is correct or not, but it seems that some of these pilots enjoy flying helicopters because of the complexity and challenge that it brings by comparison. They enjoy the feeling of controlling the aircraft rather than pushing some buttons and having the aircraft do all the work. It makes sense to me, but by the same logic I can see why Will would want to have a go at flying a paramotor. Being an integral part of the aircraft, feeling the wind on you whilst leaning into the turn and applying just the right amount of pressure to the brakes, felt much more intuitive and natural to me than endlessly trying to steady the cyclic of a helicopter.

The lesson ended with Will back at the controls, but before we came back in for the landing, it was time for Will's 'party trick' which I'm guessing he does at the end of every taster lesson. It involved dipping the nose towards the ground from a couple of hundred feet up, and rushing towards the ground, and then at the very last minute pulling up. This was followed by a very controlled landing.

I suspect that for most this would be a very exciting experience; as Will pulled it back up and under control you really felt the g-force push you into your seat, and compared to most air travel in large commercial aeroplanes this is pretty dynamic flying. Honestly though, it seemed rather tame to me. When you are used to pulling a paraglider wing, which ordinarily of course should be above your head in flight, below the horizon and you are looking down at your wing, only to then swing it the other way (AKA. wingovers) the acrobatic manoeuvring of this helicopter didn't so much as raise my heartbeat.

So have my illusions of piloting a helicopter been dashed? Partially. As the old saying goes, 'never meet your heroes', and my lasting impression of my time in control of a helicopter will unfortunately be trying to steady the cyclic handle in front of me. Should vast fortune find me in later life, then I would still get one because of the ease of transporting yourself and a few others across potentially large distances in any reasonable weather conditions. It certainly is a very useful tool for getting from A to B, but as I have remarked earlier, flying for pleasure has very little to do with arriving at your destination – it is the fun of the journey that counts!

Fly-ins and flying holidays

Peter2 was the very first to mention 'fly-ins' to me back when I was still training. It doesn't seem to take very long before most trainees are brought into the world of fly-ins as it represents both a good chance to learn from others and the ever-important social side of the sport. A fly-in is effectively just a get-together of paramotor pilots. They are often arranged online, and can be open to all or simply arranged between local pilots who already know each other. A group of pilots who routinely fly together will invite others to their field, typically arrange for a BBQ or something similar, and naturally all will bring their flying gear and enjoy lots of airtime together.

For most, this a good chance to fly in larger groups. By default, you will typically only fly with those local to you, and this being a minority sport, that won't be many pilots. Any local 'club' with more than half a dozen pilots is rare. This means that a fly-in presents the opportunity to fly with more people, and that in itself can be a challenge.

A field which ordinarily seems very large can suddenly feel rather confined when there are 15 pilots trying to lay out their wings and launch. You have to be very mindful of others around you; giving way on the field for those that have set up and are waiting to launch, finding your own 'slot' where others will give way to you, paying extra attention to those in the air above you that might want to come in to land when you are preparing to launch. As a rule, priority is always given to those already in the air – they may need to land due to an issue with their engine for example, and so those on the ground must be ever vigilant and prepared to get out of the way.

When there are many pilots all needing to share the same field, communications such as via radio become impossible to use effectively. Radio communications are highly effective across a small number of pilots, particularly in a one-to-one scenario such as a first solo flight, but imagine the chaos of 15 or more pilots sharing a common radio frequency and all talking over each other. It becomes very difficult to identify who is talking, and where they might be, and has the potential to do more harm than good.

Hence if verbal communications become useless, that really only leaves visual awareness as the means of keeping track of everyone and remaining safe. As I stated at the outset of this book, it is not my intention to write a 'how to' guide, however, considering the potential safety concerns of numerous pilots flying together, I think it would be useful to outline some methods for ensuring it works safely:

- Staggered launches. This doesn't mean that the entire group might not all be in the air at the same time, but by staggering the launch into

smaller groups you are more likely to have less confusion. Be aware of the potential for some to come into land when you are launching however!
- Flying in smaller groups. A group of 4 pilots can easily stay together in the air and keep track of the positions of each other. Across a group of 12 this can be much more challenging. Remember that when in the air there is potential for people to fly behind you, above you and below you, and so trying to ensure that you can see them, and that they can see you, becomes more challenging the more pilots there are around you.
- Flights with purposeful destinations. As a straight forward example, half the group could launch and fly West, whilst the other half fly East. Having many pilots take to the air, each with their own independent flight plans, is a dangerous proposition. The 'host' pilots should be able to recommend some interesting sights for those that are visiting, and then plan to fly a different route themselves.
- Don't fly directly above others. The majority of the time the wing is above your head; so if you are flying directly above someone, they will not be able to see you. If they decide to increase their altitude then they could fly upwards into you inadvertently.
- Don't fly directly behind others. This relates to your own safety rather than other peoples', but in flight a paragliding wing leaves rotor and turbulence behind it in its own wake. Flying through someone else 'wake' has the potential to collapse your wing, and so should be avoided.

- Don't fly low over the landing field. Those on the ground will expect that any pilot flying low is coming into land and will give you space. Flying low to wave to others or show off for example, but not land, will not endear you to your fellow pilots who are trying to anticipate your movements!

One of the unexpected benefits from fly-ins is the opportunity to meet people from all walks of life. I mentioned earlier that this sport unites a variety of different people from different backgrounds, and this is never more apparent than at a large fly-in.

I have personally met pilots who are builders, teachers, engineers, roofers, accountants, farmers, sales reps, office workers, camera men, plumbers, and those that sell aeroplanes for a living! I have met students who still live at home with their parents, those that live in council houses, and those that live in million-pound houses. There are those that drive vans through to those that drive E-Type Jaguars. 16-year olds through to 60-odd-year olds. There really isn't a 'typical' paramotor pilot.

But when we get together to share our love of flying, none of that matters. People who ordinarily probably wouldn't mix, are thrown together because of their shared love of flying and there is no friction or divide. Everyone is supportive of each other and share advice on flying techniques, different brands of equipment, and good sites to fly from.

Fly-ins are a great side to the sport which offer more than just an excuse to share a couple of beers around a fire. They can yield advice on numerous aspects of the sport, make you a safer pilot, and provides a great chance for you to learn from others.

Which leads me to Flying Holidays. I have only recently been on my first paramotoring holiday and it was a great experience, and one I would recommend. In many ways, it is an extended fly-in, but in surroundings which are new to most if not all there.

There are companies out there that specialise in taking trainees to a foreign country for a 'crash course' (hopefully not!) in paragliding or paramotoring. This is not to be confused with a flying holiday with experienced pilots. As I have explained, I personally did not do one of these courses to learn paramotoring, and so will not express too much of an opinion as to their effectiveness. I can see the benefit of travelling to a foreign country to get guaranteed flying weather, which naturally would enable much more frequent opportunities to fly. The faster pace of learning and convenience needs to be balanced against the challenges of what happens after the course is finished. Flying in your home country may present different laws or climactic conditions than that of the country you did your training in. Spending two weeks in Spain learning to fly and then coming back to the United Kingdom once you are 'trained' will be quite different and potentially daunting to a new pilot. And what of the fundamentals such as where to fly from? How does one meet local pilots to fly with? What if you need advice about which paramotor to buy and ongoing maintenance?

It was Danny who arranged our flying holiday, and our destination was southern mainland Spain. Danny knew of a suitable site which he had visited previously with log cabins next to a large lake under free airspace. This was the same site that one of the paramotor manufacturers uses as their test site and it has also played host to a number of paramotor competitions over the years.

There was sufficient room for up to 15 pilots, split across these cabins, and after most of our local club signed up to the holiday, Danny posted the remaining places on an online forum on a first come first served basis. By opening up the invite list to any pilots across the UK the resultant group was a variety of ages and experience levels.

The main question you are probably asking is "how do you transport your engine and wing over with you to a foreign country?" There are a few options, some easier than others, but for our holiday Danny and another guy called Matt hired a large van and picked up everyone's gear before boarding an overnight ferry from the UK to Spain. Once on the other side, a solid day of driving to the end destination meant that all that was left was for the remaining pilots to buy themselves some cheap flights with little more than hand luggage and hire some cars at the other side. There was clearly a lot of planning involved and a few days of travelling there and back for Danny and Matt (to which the rest of us were extremely grateful) but this was perhaps the safest option in terms of minimising any damage to our equipment in transit, and also meant that everyone could fly their own personal gear.

The second option is to break down your paramotor in to the smallest parts, clean the inside of the engine components to get rid of any combustible substances, and pack them up and put them in the hold of the aeroplane. There are clearly additional costs with asking any airline company to transport components of this nature, but perhaps the larger risk to consider is the risk of damage in transit. There is the additional burden of breaking down and rebuilding your motor at each side of the journey and this will put most people off. I have never done this personally but I know of those that have and they have had no issues. It is perhaps the easiest option if you are travelling long distances where a plane is realistically the only choice of transportation.

The third option is to rent or borrow equipment whilst you are out there. This is clearly dependant on knowing contacts in your destination and agreeing the cost of hire. Whilst this means the transport is no more complicated than any other international flight, the downside is that you may not be flying equipment that you are used to or familiar with. The wing might be a different brand, or the paramotor might have a different sized engine for example. Paramotor equipment is a little like cars; you get used to using your own, and when asked to fly / drive someone else's you feel a little alien to it at first. These are, after all, aircraft that you basically strap to your own body, so even small aspects such as ensuring the harness is correctly fitted can take some time to refine. There is also the additional risk of potentially damaging someone else's equipment. One failed launch might result in a broken propeller and whilst this would be inconvenient if it was your own, it comes with additional consequences if it belongs to someone else.

Whilst I won't divulge all of the stories that happened on our flying holiday, because as we all know *what goes on tour stays on tour*, I can tell you that I will have some great memories that will never leave me. Flying in formations, cross country flying through national park mountains, finding dead horses in the river (oh yes), flying up and down the beach a foot or two above where the white waves were crashing up onto the golden beach, and landing out further up the beach to grab a beer at the beachside bar to a stunned crowd, I think all made us feel a little like heroes.

On the last day, we were even challenged by the Guardia Civil (the military police force in Spain) and there were some concerns we might end up in a Spanish prison and miss our flights back! In the end however, I think they were just interested in seeing our equipment up close!

Flying cars?

What if I told you flying cars already exist? And not simply as some multi-million pound prototype that isn't for sale, but for little more than the cost I have outlined already for a foot-launched paramotor?

Well, in a manner of speaking, flying cars have been around for a number of years now. It may not be the futuristic imaginings of pressing a button while driving along and taking to the skies, but certainly if you have been reading this thinking, "this all sounds great but I am concerned I don't have the fitness levels for running with an engine on my back," or perhaps you have a genuine disability or injury that would prevent you from taking off and landing on your feet, a *paramotor trike* might just be the answer.

The paraglider wing remains much the same as that of a paramotor, perhaps a little larger, and the same can be said of the engine and propeller. The only difference is that the engine is mounted to a frame which sits on three wheels; I have seen four wheeled options available also but these tend to be scarcer. This means that launching can be done by simply sitting down, using the throttle to move forward sufficiently to bring the wing overhead, and then sit back and give it full throttle. The thrust from the propeller pushes you along on the wheels and once enough speed has been attained the wing will lift you into the air.

It is landings however, where the real benefits of a paramotor trike can be felt.

Landing on your feet is a hugely satisfying feeling, and one few people ever experience in their lives. I will not pretend that this isn't a benefit of this sport. However, landing *consistently* well was probably the most challenging element of flying paramotors for me personally. The wind speed, and any gusts at the time, have a great impact on your ground speed – which means that the amount of pressure that you apply to 'flare' the brakes on landing varies in each instance. Imagine the brake pressure you apply in a car when going downhill; you have to brake a little harder to that of braking on level ground or going uphill. It is a similar dynamic when flaring into wind, only in a car you can easily identify when you are travelling up or downhill whereas the wind is invisible and gusts vary. Of course, you also get exposure to thousands of braking occurrences in a typical month while driving, but only a handful of paramotor landings on average across the same period. The fewer opportunities you have of embedding a new skill, the longer it takes to truly master it. After a few years of flying, this is no longer an issue as I have amassed enough experience to intuitively 'feel' it, but I have lost count of the number of landings where I fell forwards due to an ill-judged flare. I have thankfully never hurt myself or damaged my equipment, but landings can be rough. Not to mention embarrassing.

Landing a paramotor trike, on wheels, takes away that risk. Landings can still go wrong; you can flare either far too early or too late, and take rough landings accordingly, but the impacts will be felt first through wheels and not your own body.

Danny, whom I still fly with today, has recently moved from foot launched paramotoring into flying on trikes. He chose this to preserve the health of his knees, which after years of paramotor landings coupled with working a manual profession, and his age (sorry mate, couldn't resist!), are not what they were and occasionally they give him trouble. He has migrated to flying trikes to take the pressure off his knees, and this has enabled him to continue his passion for flying for years to come; prolonging his career as a pilot.

Why then aren't more people flying trikes if they are more beneficial?

Until very recently, in the UK at least, flying a paramotor trike was legally very different to that of a foot launched paramotor. The 'foot launched' part was the vital distinction; any aircraft which was foot launched benefitted from a largely de-regulated framework. There are no licencing requirements, no logbook of hours flown, and no 'air-worthiness' assessments of the aircrafts (equivalent of a car's MOT). Trikes however, being on wheels, were not exempt from the above and consequently all of the aforementioned bureaucracy applied. Naturally then, given the choice, those that could would choose to foot launch.

In early 2017 the Civil Aviation Authority (CAA) changed the rules around paramotor trikes, having taken on board the feedback from pilots that the skills required were ultimately the same as foot launched paramotoring, and now trikes fall under the de-regulation rules. This has opened up the opportunity to fly trikes when previously the rules involved were off-putting to many.

Other reasons as to why a pilot might not choose to fly trikes are simply due to the overall size. All of the brands of trike I have seen do break down into smaller components, but this may still be the difference between the entire kit fitting into the boot of your car or not when in transit. In the air, all things being equal, a trike will be slightly slower due to the increased drag that the framework and wheels will create, and theoretically the added weight will consume a little more fuel whilst flying; but these are rather marginal disadvantages.

If the thought of running and landing with an engine strapped to your back has been putting you off until know, then don't let it. The weight of the motor does not feel half as heavy on your back as it will in your hands anyway, and I would urge you to locate your nearest instructor and try it for yourself before closing your mind to it. If however, you have old injuries or disabilities, or simply prefer the idea of sitting back and taking off rather than running, then paramotor trikes are a viable alternative that still deliver most of the benefits of standard paramotoring. You can still benefit from the de-regulations, and can still feel the wind on you as you take to the skies.

If you are curious, look into it. It could open up a whole new world.

'Adventure flying' or 'bivouac' trips

This is the name given to a relatively new type of paraglider and paramotor flying, and stems from the 'cross country' style of flying I have mentioned once or twice already.

As I have outlined, paramotors are not fast modes of transportation. The wind strength and direction makes a big difference to the resultant 'ground speed' you are travelling at; that is, as the name suggests, the speed at which you are travelling in relation to the ground. Assuming nil wind for illustrative purposes, most paramotors will not exceed 35mph and even this is using a device called a 'speed bar'.

To some, this presents a challenge rather than an obstacle. It is something of a test to take a paramotor across long distances. The term 'cross country' doesn't truly mean to travel across a country's length, but rather embark upon a long flight usually with a set destination or landmark in mind.

A cross country flight can be as humble as setting out from your field, travelling towards a castle, say 20 miles away, having a nosey around, and then the return leg back to the same field. Or it could mean travelling in a set direction until a full tank of fuel is used, landing, re-fuelling at the nearest petrol station (be sure to bring a little two stroke oil with you!) and then either continuing onwards or returning back.

You may have guessed already, but paramotors can't really be used to transport luggage or goods. An aircraft which consists of little more than strapping a harness to your body doesn't leave much room for additional space for all but the necessary. Most units will have two small zipped pouches, one either side, to hold a few items such as some oil, or wallet and keys, for example. Other than this, there is of course what you can carry on your person, which then leaves strapping items to the very frame of your motor as a final alternative.

I myself have strapped an empty fuel can around the harness straps of my motor, taken off from England and travelled into Wales as a day trip with a group of other pilots. The fuel can was effectively sitting in my lap whilst in flight, and didn't impede my flight whatsoever. Upon landing, we took our cans and walked into the neighbouring town where we had lunch, refuelled, and set off back to our original launch site again in England.

Whilst in Wales, we got chatting to some people over lunch who had travelled by car from very nearby our launch location, and it had taken them two and a half hours down the small windy roads. It had taken us only two hours by paramotor – it isn't often that paramotor's are the fastest form of transport but this goes to show that it can sometimes be the case!

If you look closely, there are places around the frame of any paramotor which can be used to strap items such as a tightly rolled sleeping bag, or tent, which do not hinder the propeller or the pilot themselves. These spaces will differ depending on the model of paramotor, but usually places such as under the seat or around the fuel tank are possible locations for storing equipment that you might need on a long trip.

It is via methods such as this that 'bivouac' trips are possible. Imagine setting off across the skies with a sleeping bag and tent attached to your motor, travelling for up to three hours on a full fuel tank, then landing, setting up camp and spending the night in a beautiful and remote spot. In the morning, you could travel (walk, or fly if there is still enough fuel) to the nearest petrol station and fill up to continue the journey.

There are a few very well known examples of just such adventures; with the annual 'Icarus Trophy' being the principal illustration of just how far such journey's can be taken. This is a 'race', by paramotor, of around 1000 miles held in the USA. This shows just what is possible on these machines when the boundaries are pushed, but not all such trips need to be that daring.

Many people have flown from one end of the UK to the other; either Lands End to John O'Groats, or the West to East 'coast-to-coast', with or without 'ground support' to aid them. Ground support, in most cases, being friends or relatives travelling by car and brining food / fuel / clothing etc. when the pilots stop to land. In this way, the pilots are experiencing the excitement and challenge of the journey, but have some backup should something go wrong.

Personally, having flown now for a few years, this is the one area I would like to develop into and explore more. In order to progress, and keep challenging myself, there are a few different options to keep my love for paramotoring fresh.

The first potential avenue would be formal competitions. These can range from tasks associated with economy (yawn!), navigation, and spot landings, through to the more exciting 'slalom racing'. Paramotor slalom racing is probably the most spectator-friendly of the competitions, as it is performed very low to the ground (or above water) and consists of a timed circuit flying around inflatable pylons. A quick internet search will amaze you if you have never seen it, but clearly there comes a greater degree of risk associated with this style of flying. Besides, I'm not sure I'm the competitive type.

A further area would be 'acro' flying. I have mentioned this already, but this is where a pilot will pull off certain acrobatic manoeuvres, usually from very high in the sky to provide the pilot with time should something go wrong, and is obviously very exciting for the pilot involved. The aim is naturally to pull off ever more daring and precise movements, and is akin to the excitement you may get from going on a large rollercoaster. This style of flying often goes hand in hand with specific 'SIV' courses, that an experienced paramotor pilot can go on to learn how to intentionally stall or deflate your wing, and the correct techniques required to correct it.

One of the guys I went to Spain with on our flying holiday had done a few of these SIV courses, and we watched him at one point perform a full stall over a lake. Essentially, this is where the pilot pulls the lines in such a manner as to collapse the wing – the wing will lose its shape and flop around until rectified. During this process, you are no longer flying but rather falling. It took maybe 10 seconds or so for this guy to recover from the stall and regain full control of the glider, but for most of us on the ground watching at the time I think this was one of the longest 10 seconds of our lives. It was not a nice feeling to watch someone place themselves in such danger, and whilst he recovered the wing completely and landed to a firm handshake from us all, I knew that this style of flying was not for me.

Lastly then, there is adventure flying, which in the manner I have described, really strikes at the heart of why I got involved in the sport in the first place, and highlights some of the advantages that this aircraft especially can provide.

In a small aeroplane, or helicopter, I couldn't land out in fields next to small towns and simply refuel using standard unleaded petrol. I would need an airport, a runway perhaps, and special aviation fuel. I couldn't simply land in an area of a National Park, without harming or disturbing the environment and wildlife around me, only to set up camp and spend the night under the stars. And if something did go wrong, perhaps a broken propeller on launch for example, I couldn't simply phone a friend to come and pick me and my aircraft up in their car.

I got involved in this sport to get airborne, to experience a sense of freedom that only flying can provide, and in short, to have adventures. Bivouac flying sums all of that up and is likely to be the area I pursue in the years to come.

Points for the budding pilot

Now that I have neared the end of my own story to date, and hopefully you have been inspired to explore the world of paramotoring for yourself, I would like to reiterate some of the lessons you can learn from my story, and in the subsequent chapter I will outline a plan for you to follow to get started.

- Accept the risks. Ensure they make you a safer pilot through diligent pre-flight checks (an instructor will show you what these are). Life presents us with risks every day whether we choose them or not! Better to face some level of acceptable risk doing something you love.

- Don't let your age hold you back! Finesse is more important than fitness. Remember 60-odd year old Trooper running off those hills, or 16-year old Katie making it look easy.

- Injuries, and certain disabilities, may not be such a road block as you might believe. Trikes can potentially open up the world of flight to you if you do not feel able to wear an engine on your back – although try this first because it is not as heavy or uncomfortable as it sounds!

- Only get tuition from an experienced and qualified instructor. I have outlined more advice on this in the next chapter.

- Don't buy equipment if you are not 100% committed. The second-hand market for flying equipment is naturally risky (you don't know how well it has been taken care of) and the chance of resale to someone you don't know and trust is slim. Do you really want to buy a second-hand wing or paramotor just to save some money? Well neither do most other people.

- The number of launches and landings are far more important than the number of hours logged. The truth is that flying these aircraft whilst in the air is very easy; pull the left handle to turn left, and pull the right handle to turn right. As such, when you are new to the sport, you are not really learning very much by spending extra time in the air. The skill, and therefore learning, really comes from launches and landings. An hour of repeatedly taking off, circling around a couple of times, and landing again, is far more useful in terms of your experience than an hour long flight with a single launch and landing.

- People mean a lot in this sport. Find people who are trustworthy and treat you like friends; if you don't get that feeling then keep looking. You will be relying on these people to help you learn a skill by which your life is potentially at risk.

- Don't feel pressured to buy the particular brand of paramotor or wing that your instructor sells.

Most instructors are 'dealers' in either wings or motors, and as such will naturally try to guide you towards buying their own brands. Do your own research. There is certainly a benefit from knowing someone with your brand of motor, in case something gets damaged for example, but they don't differ that much. If they are good people, they won't mind you buying different equipment. Just because you learnt to drive in a Ford, doesn't mean you have to buy a Ford as your first car.

- Reciprocate the favours; even if you can't help tune a carburettor, you can be courteous and help people launch, pack their wings away, give way on the field etc. I hope I can give back half of what others have done for me over the years in this sport.

- Always try to be respectful and courteous to members of the public, whether they are simply curious or making a complaint. The sport benefits from being largely de-regulated, and intentionally flying in such a manner that could jeopardise this status will not endear you to the public or your fellow pilots.

- Don't fly alone. Even if you are the only person in your area which flies one of these, after your training when you are 'going it alone', at the very least ensure that someone at home knows you are out flying. In the event of an injury you may be very grateful that someone is expecting you back by a certain time and will investigate any delay.

- Whilst training, the periods spent ground handling are the most frustrating. Push through, and don't quit. After this period, you will have access to your very own aircraft and can use it whenever the weather and your time permits. Be patient, and keep going.

- A point I struggled with, but try not to weather watch and plan your life around flying. After a couple of flights, you are likely to be 'hooked' and can't wait for the next opportunity to go and fly with your new friends. You may find yourself frustrated when there are extended periods when you can't fly due to bad weather, damaged equipment, or life's other commitments getting in the way. After years of flying I can comfortably say I have 'scratched the itch,' but I can still get irritable if I haven't flown for a few weeks in a row. Understand that *the sky will always be there.*

- Lastly, have fun!

How do I get started?

If you have read this far then you are probably ready for the next steps. You may have decided that this is something you would like to research more, but simply don't know where to start. We have all been there. I will stop trying to convince you that this might be one of the most liberating choices you may ever make, because you know this by now, and move into outlining some practical steps you can do to get started.

The first is to find your local instructor / school. To avoid any potential 'cowboys' out there that might be pilots themselves, but not have the necessary skills in teaching others, I can only recommend searching first for the *association* in your country of residence.

There are paramotoring associations all over the world although you have probably never heard of them. In the UK, the leading association is the British Hang gliding and Paragliding Association (BHPA), in the USA there is the United States Powered Paragliding Association (USPPA), and covering most of the world there is the Association of Paragliding Pilots and Instructors (APPI). There are of course others, and I would recommend either going with one of the above or another official association in your own country.

Once you have identified the appropriate association visit their website; they will have a search function which enables you to find the nearest instructor / school to you. Hopefully there will be one within a reasonable distance, but if not, and you have tried other associations (such as the global association 'APPI' mentioned above) then your only practical option will be to visit a school for an intensive 'crash course' style teaching. A quick search online for 'paramotor school...' will present a host of options in foreign countries or similar where the weather is consistently flyable. Just ensure that the instructors are registered with a reputable association.

By going through an association, you will be exposed to a structured syllabus of learning, which will likely be accompanied by some short theory exams. It is important that you know not only how to physically fly a paramotor safely, but understand the theory of flight dynamics, can identify safe conditions to fly in, and understand the applicable air laws in your country.

Another benefit from learning with an association, is that most will offer third party insurance cover; conditional on you following your instructors guidance and flying under supervision whilst you are learning. Once you have 'qualified' you can join the association yourself as a member and continue to be covered as a pilot in your own right.

I have not mentioned insurance until now, as I cynically believe that if you are learning about paramotors for the first time, and one of the first questions you are asking yourself is regarding insurance, then perhaps this sport is not for you. That may sound a little harsh, but this activity does introduce a certain element of risk into your life and it will require a certain mental outlook in order to proceed. Insurance, by its very nature, implies a certain risk averse attitude.

Naturally, given the risks involved, you are unlikely to find an insurance company that will provide a 'fully comprehensive' level of cover. If you fall over on landing and break your propeller, be prepared to buy yourself a new one rather than claim on some insurance. However, third party cover, is very possible from a number of insurers. This will cover the damages to others or their property should you, say, crash land through someone's roof. Such instances are naturally rare, which is probably why insurance companies will cover you at all. At the time of writing, AXA provided an affordable third party policy outside of any paramotoring association.

Life insurance is the other consideration. It is not impossible for you to be fatally injured whilst flying your paramotor, and that could leave your loved ones in financial difficulties if you are not covered. If you do not declare that you paraglide then the insurance companies might use that as reason not to pay out on your death. I have personally found a common life insurance provider which does cover death from paragliding at a very modest cost, although I have also been given some quotes by other companies which were extremely high. Shop around on this point, and if in doubt phone the insurance provider and outline specifically what paramotoring is and that you will only be doing this as a pastime, not as an instructor or source of income. So long as this is specifically listed in the conditions of cover then you should be fine.

So by now you should have found your local instructor or school from searching within an official association. My first recommendation would be to contact them and arrange for a time to visit in person; explain simply that you are interested in paramotoring and would like to learn more.

Suggest visiting when they next have their students learning as opposed to meeting one-on-one. This will give you the chance to find out a few things before you commit yourself to this instructor; the field that they use to teach others in (is it well kept and convenient for you to get to?), the relationships between them and their students (is there a strong rapport?), their approach to you as a potential student (do they try a 'hard sell' or are they relaxed and informative?).

Take the opportunity to speak with the students that are there; are they enjoying it? Have they bought their own equipment yet? How long have they been training? Does the instructor provide tandem flights? They won't mind you asking questions that they themselves were asking not that long ago, so be candid and get the answers you want.

At this initial meeting the instructor will probably talk you through the syllabus and structure of the training. If they don't, or they find questions of this nature difficult to respond to then beware – they should be very familiar with their structure and if not, it is a worrying sign. By structure I simply mean the order of the training; so starting at ground handling, interspersed with theory, exams perhaps, then tandem flight, then first solo flight. I personally feel that the tandem was the most valuable part of the training and I would consider this an absolute must for any training programme. You shouldn't underestimate the sensory overload of taking to the skies for the first time, and you don't want this to occur when you are the pilot in control.

Assuming all of the above is covered, and the instructor is making you feel confident in them and the standards they keep, then you have probably found a good school.

Tips on buying equipment

Whilst learning, the instructor should provide the equipment (wing, paramotor, helmet etc.) for you to learn with. They will do this until at least your first solo flight but after this it is generally expected that you buy your own equipment. There is clearly a risk for the instructor in letting you use their equipment because of any potential damages; do not however let them rush you into buying any equipment before you have gone through the training. A good instructor won't act like this in any case.

In the Tips chapter earlier, I mention the importance of doing your own research when buying equipment. To reiterate, most instructors also sell certain brands of either wing or paramotor, or indeed both. Even the most well meaning instructor will naturally try to guide you towards their particular brand, and there may be nothing wrong with the products they are selling, but make sure they meet your particular needs.

For example, perhaps you have found the weight of the motor on your back a challenge in your training to date, in which case perhaps there are brands of paramotor out there that are lighter and / or more comfortable than the brand you have learned with. Perhaps you have had difficulties with the 'hang points' for the paramotor (where the wing clips onto the motor)? Generally hang points are either 'high' which means they attach around shoulder height, or 'low' where they attach closer to your sides just above your waist. Perhaps you have been wishing the paramotor was easier and quicker to dismantle and fit in your car? Perhaps not all brands fit in your car at all?

Some distinctions you will only learn the more you are exposed to different set ups, but if there has been a particular aspect of the equipment which has bothered you then shop around – another manufacturer may have addressed your concerns and 'solved' the problem.

Let me be quite clear, in my opinion, *there is no perfect paramotor set up*. Most people will agree with this statement, as each brand will have its own unique 'strengths'. Do your research and find out what you value most.

To help, the following is a list of paramotor manufacturers that you could look into. There will definitely be more out there so these are only the ones I know of, and to be clear, I am not affiliated with any company or brand of paramotor or wing. In no particular order, some different brands of paramotor are:

- PAP
- Air Conception
- Parajet
- Bailey
- Bulldog

- Scout
- Blackhawk
- Fresh Breeze

Hopefully the above will get your started and you can start to identify the pro's and con's.

In terms of paramotor wings, I would advise *against* buying an outright 'beginner' (EN-A certified) wing. This may sound controversial, but most experienced pilots will suggest the same if they are being honest with you.

As I have explained already, the rating of a wing is effectively a trade off between passive safety and speed / handling. As a beginner you will want a lot of passive safety, so that should you fly through turbulence then you can trust the wing will take care of you. This would lead you towards an EN-A rated wing, but the problem is that these are generally so slow and docile that you will quickly outgrow it.

Even a new beginner wing will cost you over £2,000 which is roughly the same price as an EN-B Intermediate wing. Given the cost of a wing, you are likely to want to get years of use out of it before replacing it, which means if you buy an EN-A rated wing then you are somewhat stuck with it for a few years. During those early years your experience will grow very quickly, as with any new skill, and you risk being left with a wing that isn't allowing your skills to progress accordingly.

The launch, landing and flight characteristics of an EN-B Intermediate wing are not very different to that of a beginner wing, yet an Intermediate wing can last you much longer. It goes without saying that I do not recommend buying an EN-C or higher wing – these are generally for competition pilots and should only be considered after years of solid experience.

I personally have always flown an EN-B wing, and I don't envisage ever flying anything else. I have no interest in competing, and the speed I can attain on my wing is fast enough to keep up with friends when travelling on 'cross-country' long distance flights. They still however provide a strong level of passive safety and don't require active pilot input should something go wrong – in most instances they 'fix' themselves without active piloting and the only measurable difference between this and a beginner wing is the time it takes for the 'fix' to happen – and we are talking a matter of seconds here.

The only other thing I might mention are 'reflex' wings. This is the term used to describe when the wing can automatically alter its pitch and profile in order to 'smooth out' turbulent air. What this means is that they are safer and require less active flying from the pilot. An instructor will be able to explain this in more detail. Nowadays, most wings have some level of 'reflex' in them and it seems an easy decision to my mind to choose one.

Again, to get you started, here is a list of some of the more common paramotor wing manufacturers:

- Apco
- Niviuk
- Ozone
- Paramania
- Dudek

In my opinion, there are fewer differences between the brands of wings (of the same EN rating) than for paramotors, and most of the below brands will use superlative language to describe their own products. Just be mindful of the rating of the wing when choosing, and don't fall for over-zealous 'brand loyalty'. I am very happy with my current set up, but I will be trying other brands in the future. Just because I drive a Honda now, doesn't mean I will only drive a Honda for the rest of my life.

Final thoughts

Most people don't realise personal flight is within their reach; restricted to the realms of adrenaline junkies with a death wish or multi-millionaires who travel by personal jets. This could not be further from the truth. A dream for the ancients, which can be fulfilled in today's world with only a little hard work and investment; personal, affordable flight is well within the reach of most people.

In my experience, paramotoring draws a great variety of different people from varied backgrounds. I am pleased to say that almost all the people I have met in this sport are helpful, respectful, and genuinely encouraging and supportive of others fulfilling their dreams.

Throughout this book I have referred to paramotoring, and flight in general, as either a pastime or a sport. I would take this opportunity, now you have heard my story to date, to correct this term.

A pastime it certainly isn't; this isn't something to do to help flitter away our precious life because there isn't anything better to do with our time.

Whilst there are competitions out there in the paramotoring world, I don't think it is truly fair to call it a sport either. Sport implies competition -

with winners and losers. I have never seen any competition in paramotoring. On the contrary, I have seen people helping, educating and looking out for each other. We all feel like winners, no matter how advanced or skilful we are. We are fulfilling our dreams which most of us have had since childhood, but never really believed we could achieve.

I would, therefore, rename paramotoring from a pastime or sport to *a life-enhancing activity*.

I am so very pleased that I decided to make that first phone call to Peter1 all those years ago. I am grateful for the set-backs and injuries I have sustained because they have made me a better pilot. I am appreciative of the great friends I have made along the journey. And most of all, I am thrilled with the adventures yet to come.

If you have ever wanted to fly, to get in the air and taste the freedom it brings, then I urge you to follow this book up with action. Don't put it off. Don't let your fitness concerns, age or fears put you off. Research it at least. It might not be for you; but at least you will have answered that question for yourself.

Who knows, maybe we will see each other in the air some time.

Printed in Great Britain
by Amazon